Ford Nation

Ford Nation

Why hundreds of thousands of Torontonians supported their conservative crack-smoking mayor

Arthur Weinreb

ISBN: 1508525250
ISBN 13: 9781508525257
Library of Congress Control Number: 2015902617
CreateSpace Independent Publishing Platform
North Charleston, South Carolina

Table of Contents

Introduction

Thousands of books have and are still being written about how to make money on the stock market. And they all say the same thing—buy when it's low and sell when it's high. It is such a simple principle children first learning about arithmetic are able to grasp its meaning. So why isn't everyone who invests in the market, rich?

The reality is that while everyone understands the principle of buying low and selling high, most people don't do it. They think that is what they are doing but in actual fact they are buying when the price is high and hoping like hell it will go higher.

And so it is with conservatism. Conservatives know when candidates and elected politicians stay true to their small "c" conservative principles, they do very well. Ronald Reagan, Margaret Thatcher and former Ontario Premier Mike Harris are examples of not only campaigning on conservative principles but of governing as small "c" conservatives. Although this is a simple principle like the stock market example, many conservatives do not follow through. They think if they water down their principles, their party will attract more members and their candidates more votes. During the current race for the leadership of the Ontario Progressive Conservative Party, perceived front-runner Christine Elliott began her campaign by announcing she was going to make the PCs a "big tent party." What did she mean by that? The party will let gays and lesbians in? Jews? Blacks? No, what Elliott meant is that she wants the

PCs to attract members who are not conservatives. There is room for everybody including disenchanted Liberals.

The problem is this doesn't work. By moving to the centre and welcoming progressives and others who lean left into their fold, the party will be praised by liberals and the media for being centrist. But when the next election comes, voters will turn to the real thing and vote for the Liberals or the socialist NDP. The media that complimented the party on its centrist approach will turn on them when the next election is called and endorse the real left of centre parties.

Robert Bruce Ford, the 64th mayor of the city of Toronto is an unabashed fiscal conservative. Social policies do not really enter into the municipal political sphere. Although we know Ford has never marched in a Gay Pride parade, we do not really know how he stands on many social issues. It is his obsession with not wasting other peoples' money on spending that benefited only special interest groups or the councillors themselves that endeared him to members of Ford Nation. His willingness to help constituents personally, even after becoming mayor, and his ability to relate to ordinary people, coming across as just being "one of them," also created a large following of those who stayed with him despite allegation after allegation, scandal after scandal.

Although the *Toronto Star* endorsed Ford when he made his first successful electoral bid in 2000 and was elected as councillor in Ward 2, the left wing media were on him almost from the outset. They made fun of his buffoonish behaviour and lamented how the city would be destroyed if spending was limited as he suggested. It was the spin that we see so often in the United States; like Republicans, if Ford ever came to power, children would starve to death, the elderly would die, and life as we know it would end.

Despite the harsh criticism levelled against him by the elites, compounded when new allegations emerged and culminated in the crack scandal, Ford never deviated from his core beliefs on fiscal conservatism. Never once did he moderate his views in order to attempt to get the media and those on the centre left to like him in an attempt to broaden his base of support. When evidence began to emerge about his substance abuse, his homophobic, racist and anti-Semitic comments and council voted to take away as much of his power as they could, many people believed it was only a matter of time before he resigned. A lot of politicians have given up their offices after doing or being accused of a lot less. But those who knew him knew he would never quit in the face of a barrage of criticism that by 2013 was tantamount to bullying. He stayed in office and stayed on message, determined as ever to stop the gravy train.

Only a cancer diagnosis would see him drop out of the 2014 mayor's race. Even then he decided to run for his old council seat and he won it easily despite the fact he was only in the race for six weeks of the 10-month campaign and was only seen in public between chemotherapy treatments when he felt up to it.

While his enemies describe Ford Nation as a cult, many of those who supported him throughout the 2014 campaign did so because he never wavered on his brand of fiscal conservatism. While others campaigned on issues of reducing spending on council, no other politician, with the exception of his brother Doug, ever came close to approximating his enthusiasm on city council's excessive spending.

The more Ford was criticized, the more he stuck to his guns. While this spurned a city of Ford-haters, it also created a group of people whose admiration of Ford grew as he continued in office despite worsening scandals. While members of Ford Nation have been and are written off as knuckle-dragging Neanderthals, they are a legitimate force in the city of Toronto that should not be ignored.

Rob Ford's story is a story about how a dedicated fiscal conservative could attract and keep a strong base of support in the face of allegations and scandals that would have made most others leave office in disgrace. Ford is a man who is obsessed with saving the money of the overtaxed ordinary Torontonians. And these residents remained loyal to Ford despite the fact he became a laughingstock not only in Toronto but around the world.

He is without a doubt, the most famous municipal elected official in the world. He tried to save the taxpayers' money, and he paid no attention what the left, the elites or the media thought about it. The ordinary person was his only concern.

Part I – Rob Ford – Policies, Campaigns and Scandals

Chapter 1

Toronto Mayor David Miller, 2004– 2010

In order to understand how Rob Ford was elected in the November 2010 municipal election to become the 64th mayor of the city of Toronto, it is necessary to examine his predecessor. It is highly unlikely Ford would have had any chance of winning except for Mayor David Miller's disastrous second term.

Miller was born in England in 1958 and emigrated to Canada with his mother in 1967. Mother and son moved to Toronto in 1981.

Despite being raised by a single parent, the future mayor of Canada's largest city obtained an economics degree from Harvard University and a law degree from the University of Toronto. He was first elected to Metro Council in the old city of Toronto in 1994.

When Toronto proper and the surrounding areas of Scarborough, Etobicoke, North York and East York amalgamated in 1997 in what is now the city of Toronto, Miller was elected as councillor in a ward in the city's west end. He was re-elected in the following municipal election held in 2000.

Miller was everything Ford was not; a university graduate with two degrees including one from the prestigious Harvard University, a polished lawyer who practised with a large Toronto firm prior to entering politics, and perhaps most importantly, a member of the socialist NDP although he allowed his membership to lapse in 2007 to appear more "neutral."

The married father of small children was scandal-free when it came to his personal life.

A memorable event from Miller's second term as councillor occurred when then Mayor Mel Lastman told the two-time councillor that he was too stupid to be mayor. Lastman was wrong.

Prior to the 2003 election, the city had gone through what is known as the MFP Scandal. In the late 1990s, the city had a $43 million contract with MFP Financial Services that included the sale and leaseback of computers. Without proper procedures having taken place and without the knowledge of the city, the contract ballooned to over $85 million. A judicial inquiry began in 2002 and a report subsequently issued in 2005. There was evidence of payments by an MFP employee to a sitting councillor and the finding of a sexual relationship between the city treasurer and a computer software consultant.

A police investigation was conducted and in 2010, the Ontario Provincial Police announced no criminal charges would be laid.

Miller was one of two sitting Toronto city councillors who pushed for the investigation of the dealings between the city and MFP. In the aftermath of the beginning of the judicial inquiry, the two-term councillor threw his hat into the ring and announced he would run for mayor in 2003. Holding a broom high over his head, a symbol of his campaign, Miller ran on the platform that if elected, he would clean up city hall. Another major issue Miller campaigned on was to stop the construction of a bridge to the island airport. Many downtown residents hated the fact of an airport on an island close to where they lived, let alone a bridge to make it easier to fly in and out of the city.

After the polls closed on Nov. 10, 2003, Miller ended up with 299,385 votes. His closest rival, John Tory, who ran again in 2014, ended up with 263,189 votes. Barbara Hall, who served as mayor of the pre-amalgamated old city of Toronto between 1994 and 1997, came a distant third capturing only 63,751 votes.

Miller denied his NDP roots and had campaigned as a centrist. He encountered no major difficulties in his first three-year-term as mayor. As mayor, he managed to have the bridge to the island airport stopped. And there were no major scandals such as the one involving MFP that took place during the administration of Mayor Lastman and that was played out constantly in the media. Miller had promised to hold the increase in property taxes to the rate of inflation. During his first term, taxes increased by a rate of 3%, slightly above the inflation rate but it did not seem to have a negative impact on the mayor as the 2006 election loomed.

There was nothing that could be deemed a crisis during Miller's first term and he decided to run for re-election in 2006. Under Ontario law, the term elected municipal officials held office was increased from three years to four, beginning with the 2006 election.

The election took place on November 13, 2006 and Miller won easily, capturing 332,969 votes, slightly less than 57% of the total votes cast. Jane Pitfield, a former city councillor, came second garnering 188,932 votes, a little less than one third of the total. The only other person in the race considered to be a major candidate, former Liberal Party of Canada president Stephen LeDrew, came a distant third capturing 8,078 votes.

Shortly after the November 2006 election, the city ran into financial difficulties. Under new budget chief Shelley Carroll, who replaced the somewhat conservative David Socknaki, homeowners were subjected to a 3.8% tax increase in 2007. But it was the implementation of brand new taxes that ultimately led not only to Miller's decision not to run for a third term in 2010, but which led to the significant victory of the city's next mayor, Rob Ford.

Miller was able to get the provincial liberal government to pass the *City of Toronto Act* that gave more powers to the city to tax its residents who had already seen their property taxes rise more than promised.

Ontario imposes both a vehicle registration fee and a land transfer tax on its residents. Car owners must pay a yearly fee to legally operate their vehicles and homeowners are taxed on the value of their homes when they sell their property to another party. Using the new powers under the *City of Toronto Act*, Miller and city council imposed new taxes on Toronto residents in the form of municipal land transfer taxes and vehicle registration taxes. These new taxes were of course in addition to similar fees and taxes already payable to the province. While those in other areas paid one tax, Toronto residents had to pay twice for the same thing.

In 2008, city council brought in a city vehicle registration tax. Vehicle owners were required to pay $60 a year to register a car and $30 a year for a motorcycle. During the same year, council passed the Municipal Land Transfer Tax (MLTT) with the amount of the tax dependent upon the value of the home involved. A percentage of 0.5% was payable on the first $55,000 of the sale price and 1.0% of the price between $55,000 and $400,000. The additional cost of a home over $400,000 was taxed at 2.0%. For example, the additional tax on a home sold for $500,000, not an unusual amount in Toronto at that time, was $5,725.

The fact that these were not only increased or new taxes but the same taxes imposed by the province, requiring Torontonians to pay twice while other Ontarians paid once, angered many taxpayers. The imposition of these cash grabs marked the beginning of the end of Mayor David Miller.

To make things worse, these new taxes failed to bring in the amount of revenue the city estimated they would. During the first year, the MLTT, estimated to bring in $300 million, raised only slightly more than half that amount ($155 million). The city cried it was the fall in the real estate market led to the shortfall. The vehicle registration tax netted Toronto $13.5 million, far less than the projected $20 million.

The bright lights in the city of Toronto figured out people used the addresses of friends, relatives or other property they owned outside of Toronto as the address to register their vehicles, enabling them to avoid the additional tax. It was not a good sign for either Miller or the city.

Into his second term, Miller could no longer pretend he was a centrist whose main goal was to clean up scandals and city hall. He showed he was a tax-and-spend leftist with no real thought about how his spending affected the less well-off taxpayers in the city. With the global meltdown that began in 2008, it wasn't getting any easier for a lot of people to survive financially.

Miller also began getting involved in issues that were not strictly municipal issues. The final year of the mayor's first term was referred to as "The year of the gun." That year saw numerous killings including the slaying of 15-year-old Jane Creba. Creba was shopping with family members on Toronto's main drag, Yonge Street, on Boxing Day, the busiest shopping day of the year when she was caught in a crossfire between rival gang members and shot to death.

In the spring of 2008, Miller backed a bylaw that would ban the manufacturing and the keeping of guns in the city. The regulation of firearms falls within the jurisdiction of the federal government and no one was going to be any safer if guns were stored or manufactured in the 'burbs rather than the city proper. This was in addition to the obvious fact this was aimed at the law abiding residents of Toronto and legitimate gun manufacturers; criminals who don't worry about committing crimes that can lead to incarceration were not about to be deterred by a city bylaw. The mayor had come a long way since he was first elected in 2003.

Like all leftist governments in the West, Miller was concerned with climate change or as it was called before near record cold temperatures began to emerge, global warming. Like these other governments, Toronto began a program of "greening" the city. But Miller, an environmental activist, went further.

In 2008, Miller was appointed chair of the C40, a group of cities throughout the world tasked to tackling climate change. Miller's spokesman told the media that the honour of chairing the group came with "certain obligations." These obligations cost money; not Miller's of course but money from taxpayers who in addition to tax increases higher than inflation, new vehicle registration and land transfer taxes, were caught in the general downturn of the economy.

During 2009 budget deliberations, the budget included $140,000 for the C40 group. This was in addition to the $70,000 the city paid the year before in order to staff the office of the C40 located in London, England. Despite levying new taxes and raising existing taxes and user fees, the mayor justified this expense as necessary to save the planet. Many people were not impressed.

It is difficult to know if Miller could have won a third term despite the additional taxes and his preoccupation with using Torontonians' money to stop global warming and fighting other non-municipal causes. But an event took place during the summer of 2009 that made even the downtown tax and spend liberals angry.

The left wing Miller made no secret that he owed his main loyalty to the city workers whose unions backed him. During much of 2009, the city was negotiating with the two Canadian Union of Public Employees (CUPE) unions representing inside and outside city workers. The unresolved issue, in addition to money of course, was the ability of workers to bank sick days. Despite his friendliness with the unions representing Toronto's workers, an agreement was unable to be reached regarding sick days.

At midnight on June 22, 2009, both unions representing about 30,000 city workers went on strike. While many of the services provided by these workers have little or no impact on the day to day lives of average Torontonians, the loss of other services such as parks being cleaned and swimming pools remaining open caused only minor inconveniences. But what irked Toronto residents the most was the lack of garbage collection.

The strike was finally settled after 36 days. The *Globe and Mail* reported the final offer the unions accepted was the most generous offer made public throughout the strike. The contract was to last three years and not the four Miller initially wanted. Workers were to get wage increases of 6% over three years instead of the earlier proposed 4%.

Under the previous contract, workers were entitled to bank up to 18 sick days and then cash them out when they retire. Only new employees would be prevented from banking these sick days while existing workers were given several options of cashing in their existing days. The settlement cost.

But it was the stench of rotting garbage throughout the city during the hot summer months that made Toronto residents the angriest. While some people could choose to keep their garbage at home until the strike was over, temporary dump sites were set up in Toronto parks and other sites where people could take their refuse. There were horror stories of incidents between the striking workers and residents who felt they were delayed an inordinate amount of time before they were allowed to dump their garbage. The longer the strike went on, the more the garbage stank, especially for those people who lived near these temporary dump sites.

A poll taken during the strike showed Miller's popularity had plummeted. The golden haired boy's approval rating, at 69% in early 2009, dropped to 43% as the work stoppage progressed. Over half the people polled (57%) said the city was moving in the wrong direction.

On Sept. 25, 2009, Miller announced he would not be seeking a third term in 2010. He gave the usual excuse made by politicians who quit or say they will not run again because they see the writing on the wall — he wanted to leave politics to spend more time with his family.

With tax increases, new taxes, and the smell of the garbage freshly in residents' minds, the time was ripe for Rob Ford's message of "respect for taxpayers," and "stopping the gravy train."

Chapter 2

The 2010 Toronto Municipal Election Campaign

Who can run for the office of mayor or municipal councillor is determined by provincial law and the requirements are not onerous. To be a candidate to lead Canada's largest city, a person must be a Canadian citizen and reside in Toronto. The potential candidate must pay a minor fee to enter the race; for the 2014 election, it was $200. The only other qualification is the candidate cannot be in jail. Criminal records, convictions or outstanding charges do not pose barriers to running for and holding elected office. As far as crimes go, a person is not ineligible to run or hold office until the steel doors slam shut and the cavity search begins.

There are always numerous mayoral candidates in Toronto and during the past election campaign in 2014, over 60 people registered to run. These include those who run during every election campaign and single issue candidates who feel their position on that single issue will save the city, if not the world. There are always entertaining candidates and in 2014 these included a clown and a dominatrix who ran on the platform of whipping the city into shape.

The candidates are divided into three categories and this is largely dependent upon how these people are treated by the media. The top group are those high profile candidates who are well known and who have, at least initially, a chance to win. The second tier candidates are those who are known for their political or other past endeavours but who are long shots when it comes to actually winning. Those that are running simply because they want to and could come up with the cash to register, comprise the third category.

During the 2010 campaign, there were three major candidates for the office; George Smitherman, a former Ontario Liberal cabinet minister and councillors Rob Ford and Joe Pantalone.

The second tier ended up being composed of two people; Sarah Thomson and Rocco Rossi. Thomson is the publisher and CEO of the magazine, *Women's Post*, and an entrepreneur who had married into the prominent Thomson family. Being a second-tier candidate meant she was invited to participate in the numerous debates and was given some attention by the media. Although the unsuccessful candidate also ran in the 2014 election before dropping out, she was dropped to the third tier in 2014 alongside the clown and the dominatrix. Back in 2010, the overly politically correct media needed a woman candidate despite the fact since 1990, Toronto has had two female mayors, June Rowlands and Barbara Hall. The necessity of Thomson as a token woman was not necessary in 2014 since NDP MP and former councillor Olivia Chow and Councillor Karen Stintz were both running.

Rocco Rossi was a businessman and later became the CEO of the Heart and Stroke Foundation. Rossi also served for a time as the national director of the Liberal Party of Canada.

Both of these second-tier candidates dropped out prior to Election Day. Thomson threw her support to Smitherman while Rossi declined to say who he was supporting.

Pantalone was the most experienced of the candidates. A progressive, he had served on both Toronto City Council and the now abolished Metro Council for over 30 years. He also served for a time as deputy mayor under Miller. An NDP member, Pantalone never stood much of a chance and finished a distant third in the race. Despite his experience he was much too closely aligned with Miller to be a successful candidate, at least in 2010. During his last term in office, Pantalone served as Toronto's "Tree Advocate."

The race was essentially a two-way race between Ford and Smitherman. And Ford, who was never taken seriously by the elites since he was first elected as councillor in 2000, was thought to stand pretty well no chance of winning. It was obvious to the lefties and the elites that George Smitherman was going to be the next mayor of Toronto. But as they always do, the voters had something to say about that.

George Smitherman

Smitherman grew up in Etobicoke where he attended high school. Although he later liked to talk about his humble roots (his father was a truck driver) he did not talk much about the fact he was a high school dropout.

Smitherman became active in politics in high school and became active in the Liberal Party of Ontario. He worked as an executive assistant to MPP Hugh O'Neill and as an advisor to federal Liberals David Collenette and Herb Gray.

Smitherman also had experience in municipal politics in Toronto when he served as chief of staff to Mayor Barbara Hall.

In 1999, Smitherman ran provincially in a liberal downtown Toronto riding. Despite the fact the Progressive Conservatives obtained their second straight majority government under Premier Mike Harris that year, Smitherman won the riding of Toronto Centre. He was the first openly gay man to be elected to the legislature and later became the first openly gay cabinet minister.

In 2003, the provincial Liberals won a majority government and shortly after coming to power, Premier Dalton McGuinty appointed Smitherman to the cabinet where he served as Minister of Health and Long Term Care. During his term in the provincial legislature, he served in the health portfolio and in 2008, became the Minister of Energy and Infrastructure.

In the legislature, Smitherman was known as McGuinty's attack dog or pit bull and was constantly referred to as "Furious George." His ability to strongly attack McGuinty's opponents led him to be appointed Deputy Premier of Ontario. It was quite a feat for a high school dropout.

Smitherman endured scandals while in cabinet although the scandals hardly put a dent in the popularity of the Liberals in Ontario. While

Smitherman did not hold the health portfolio during the entire time these scandalous events had taken place, he was associated with them.

An outbreak of C. difficile occurred in Ontario hospitals during the 2000s and 264 people died during that outbreak. In 2008, Smitherman, as health minister, refused to call a public inquiry into the deaths, saying it was not necessary despite the recommendation by the province's ombudsman, Andre Marin, that such an inquiry should be held. Smitherman's refusal came shortly before he was moved to his new portfolio but he refused to acknowledge his handling of the C. difficile file had anything to do with McGuinty's decision to remove him from the health ministry.

Another scandal to come under the auspices of the Ministry of Health was that of Ornge. Although the province had had an air ambulance service since 1977, a new body was created under Smitherman's watch in 2005. It was called Ornge after the colour of its aircraft and the new body was a non-for-profit enterprise tasked with coordinating medical air transportation throughout the province.

Although Smitherman was long gone before the scandal emerged, he was associated with it by virtue of his being the Minister of Health when the organization came into being. A report on Ornge was due to be released in May, 2014, but not released after Premier Kathleen Wynne's decision to dissolve the legislature and call an election. Since the Liberals refused to release the report, the opposition Progressive Conservatives did.

The report found wrongdoing at the highest levels of the ministry in the areas of management, health and safety risks. Board members of Ornge were found to have breached their financial duties, were paid exorbitant amounts of money and executives of Ornge were accused of siphoning off government monies to private companies they had interests in. The governing Liberals blamed Ornge itself for "going rogue" and took no real responsibility even though health and safety charges were laid and a police investigation initiated. Losses to the taxpayers were in the millions.

The largest scandal during the Smitherman years was that of eHealth. EHealth was a program designed to put Ontarians health records online. A report of the auditor general, released in October 2009, indicated about $1 billion of the taxpayers' money was wasted. Millions of dollars were spent on computer systems that were never used and generous untendered contracts awarded to consultants. After the waste of all this money, the health records of Ontario residents were never completely put online.

After the report came out, both opposition parties demanded Smitherman's resignation although he was now in the energy and infrastructure portfolio. Smitherman refused to resign and the premier did not ask him to resign from cabinet. McGuinty however took responsibility for the eHealth fiasco.

On November 8, 2009, a month after the latest scandal involving his portfolio emerged, Smitherman announced he was not only resigning his cabinet position but would resign as an MPP effective Jan. 4, 2010. He was planning to run for mayor of Toronto.

Rob Ford

Like Smitherman, Ford grew up in Etobicoke. Unlike Smitherman, Ford actually graduated from high school and spent a year at Carleton University in Ottawa before dropping out. Ford wanted to play professional football and although he made the Carleton football team, he did not get to play.

Ford's father, Doug Sr., founded Deco Label and Tags in 1962. The company manufactures special pressurized labels and tags and is one of the leading companies of its kind in North America. The company does hundreds of millions of dollars in sales annually and has locations in Toronto, Chicago and New Jersey. After Ford dropped out of university, he went to work in the family business in sales.

Doug Sr. was also involved in politics and sat as an MPP for the Progressive Conservative Party of Ontario under Mike Harris between 1995 and 1999, representing a riding then known as Etobicoke-Humber.

Rob Ford first tried his hand in politics by making an unsuccessful run for city councillor in 1997. He ran in Etobicoke's Ward 3 and finished fourth. He obtained 9,366 votes in a campaign that saw Gloria Lindsay Luby win the seat with 13,123 votes.

Ford tried again in 2000, this time in Ward 2. He won, beating the incumbent councillor Elizabeth Brown by more than 1,500 votes. The future mayor easily won re-election in 2003 and 2006.

When Ford gave up his seat to run for mayor in 2010, his brother Doug ran in the ward and won.

After taking his seat on city council, the rookie councillor wasted no time in setting the tone for what his years as councillor and later mayor would look like. He was bombastic and prone to rants on the council floor. In early 2001, he said what would later become one of his mantras; that the city did not have a revenue problem, it had a spending problem.

Ford mainly railed against the expenses incurred by city councillors in their office budgets that were then set at $53,100 per year. Ford complained about other costs at city hall such as the limousines that all 44 councillors had access to, the cost of watering plants at Toronto City Hall and the free food provided to councillors during their meetings. This did not endear him to his fellow councillors, many of whom spent their office budgets on questionable things such as Councillor Sandra Bussin did. In a rare occurrence in municipal politics, Bussin was an incumbent who was handily defeated by an unknown challenger in the 2010 election. One of the reasons for residents in her ward voting her out was the fact she rented a bunny suit to wear in an Easter parade. And the taxpayers paid over $200 for the rental.

While going on about the excessive spending of their office budgets by some of the councillors would not have put a dent in the city's money problems, it was popular with not only Ford's constituents but with residents in other parts of the city. The rookie councillor was looking out for their interests.

Other than his constituents, Ford never cared what anybody else, his fellow councillors and the media included, thought about him. He was only interested in helping not only the people in his ward but all Torontonians, the ordinary people. This attitude of not caring what his critics, including the media, thought or said about him, allowed him to continue in office after being plagued by allegations of substance abuse and of improper behaviour related to the offices he held.

As soon as he was elected to council, Ford began a practise few in any other politicians engage in. He would hand out business cards with his cellphone number on it, telling people he met they could always contact him. When they did, he would do what he could to help them. For example if someone living in subsidized housing had a problem, Ford would go out to see it for himself and would often take someone from the city staff to attempt to remedy the situation. This made him extremely popular with the Torontonians, most of whom had representatives they could not communicate with in person or whose offices never returned phone calls.

When word got around about his cellphone number being freely available, residents living in other wards who felt they could not get help from their own councillors would call him. Ford would return their calls and help them in the same manner he did with his own constituents. Other councillors got angry whenever Ford showed up in their wards to help to solve problems they were supposed to take care of. But that did not stop the future mayor from assisting these people.

Returning phone calls and visiting Toronto residents was a practise he kept up even after being elected mayor and he was criticized for spending time as chief magistrate to go to the homes of residents to check out complaints. After he was hospitalized with cancer in his abdomen and recovering from rounds of chemotherapy, he passed the time by returning Torontonians' telephone calls.

While many councillors spent the bulk of their council office expenses, some approaching the upper limit, Ford often submitted zero expenses. In years he did file expenses, they were under $10. As an example, one year Ford submitted expense claims less than $10 were for making photocopies. The copier at Ford's family business had broken down and he was forced to go to Kinkos to make the copies he needed.

In 2007 some councillors were so upset at Ford's lack of spending the taxpayers' money they made a complaint to the city's integrity commissioner, David Mullan. A complaint was also made against Councillor Doug Holyday who was council's second lowest spender behind Ford.

The office of the integrity commissioner was set up in the wake of the MFP scandal. One function of the commissioner is to investigate complaints made against members of council to determine if the city's code of conduct had been breached.

The complaint was made by leftist members of council who thought it wasn't fair that wealthy people like Ford and Holyday did not have to account for spending if they used their own money while those councillors who needed or wanted to use their taxpayer funded budgets did.

Mullan ultimately ruled councillors had to report the amounts they spent for their office regardless of whether they used city funds or spent their own money.

To fiscal conservatives who were sick and tired of seeing their tax monies wasted by elected officials in all levels of government, criticizing politicians because they spent too little of other peoples' money seemed absurd. This particular practice earned Ford a lot of fans.

While the crack scandal did not emerge until his third year as mayor of Toronto, Ford's years on council were not scandal free. One involving alcohol occurred in 2006 and in retrospect was an indication that the councillor may have had a substance abuse problem, at least with alcohol.

In April of that year, Ford was at the Air Canada Centre to see a hockey game between the Toronto Maple Leafs and the Ottawa Senators. Towards the end of the game, a couple who were visiting from out of town said a person behind them was becoming loud and obnoxious. When the man turned around to tell him to quiet down, Ford became belligerent, swearing and making comments that were hard to understand. The future mayor was removed from the building by ACC security.

The couple later made a complaint to the office of the city clerk. Ford initially denied he was at the game but too many people in attendance had recognized him. And at the game he conducted his usual practice of handing out business cards to those around him. Ford later apologized and said he lied because he was drunk and too embarrassed to admit what he did. It was an excuse for lying he would use again.

A formal complaint was made to the integrity commissioner who ruled he had no jurisdiction over what Ford did or did not do at the Air Canada Centre.

Ford always loved football and spent his council years coaching high school football, first at Newtonbrook Secondary School and later at Don Bosco Catholic Secondary School in Etobicoke. In 2001, shortly after taking his seat he was asked to leave Newtonbrook after it was alleged he got into an altercation with one of his players. The following year he began coaching at Don Bosco and continued there until the crack scandal emerged in the spring of 2013 when he was told he was no longer needed.

Ford was criticized by many councillors and Torontonians for missing council sessions including key votes while he was both councillor and mayor to attend football practices and games. The irony is that while at Don Bosco, Ford was coaching what the left likes to call "disadvantaged youth." These are the young people these councillors seek more and more public money for in order to keep out of trouble. But the left never gave Ford credit for helping these youths who, were it not for football, might otherwise have gotten into trouble.

After gaining office, Ford soon gained a reputation for using what would be considered to be unparliamentary language. He referred to Councillor Lindsay Luby, the woman who defeated him in the 1997 election, as a "waste of skin". And he called fellow Etobicoke councillor Georgio Mammoliti a "weasel', a 'scammer', and a "goon". Ford was always getting complaints about how he talked about or referred to his fellow councillors.

Ford, both in his comments about other councillors as well as the issues of the day was never politically correct. While his statements were shocking to those on the left to whom political correctness is an absolute must, others who tend to disapprove of having to be politically correct all the time, became more supportive of the mayor.

Ford was accused of making racist and homophobic statements long before videos of the mayor in one of his drunken stupors ever surfaced. Councillor Mammoliti accused Ford of calling him a "Gino boy," an allegation Ford denied. When a discussion of the transgendered was taking place during a meeting of council, Ford asked if that was a boy who dressed as a girl or a girl who dressed as a boy.

Council had already been providing wine to alcoholics who stayed in city run residences and were debating whether to distribute safe crack kits to drug users. Ford, in what now seems ironic because of the later revelation of his own substance abuse problems, decried these programs as enabling those who are addicted to drugs.

As to AIDS, the future mayor opined if people didn't use drugs, they probably wouldn't get the disease.

Once, while trying to pay a compliment to the city's Asian population, Ford said Orientals were taking over because they "work like dogs." He said he meant it as a compliment that these people are hard workers but the politically correct crowd didn't see it that way.

If Ford did anything in his three terms as Ward 2 councillor, it was to keep the integrity commissioner busy.

Although Ford had dropped hints he would run for mayor as early as 2008, he formally registered to run in March 2010. Even to some of his supporters, it was hard to see how the scrappy, outspoken, sometimes crude council veteran of 10 years could ever win the mayor's race and lead Canada's largest city.

Formal registration to run for municipal office opened on Jan. 4, 2010. As the incumbent mayor of Toronto decided to not run again, the campaign attracted a number of high profile candidates including Rocco Rossi, Sarah Thomson and Councillors Adam Giambrone and Georgio Mammoliti. One by one they dropped out either because of a sex scandal (Giambrone) or when it was apparent they would not be able to get enough support to come close to being elected mayor (Rossi, Thomson and Mammoliti). Although Pantalone stuck it out until the end he never had a chance. Toronto's tree advocate was just too close to the outgoing Miller to ever have a chance of winning following the disastrous last term of the Harvard graduate. From the outset it was really a race between Smitherman and the three term Etobicoke councillor. And initially, the smart money was on Smitherman. The buffoonish Ford couldn't possibly win.

As an attempt to reduce the size of government, Premier Mike Harris legislated the amalgamation of the city of Toronto with the Borough of East York and the cities of North York, Etobicoke and Scarborough. There was a noticeable divide between the old city of Toronto and the suburbs, a difference that played a major role in not only the 2010 election but in the one held in 2014 and will be a factor in upcoming municipal contests.

For lack of a better definition, the downtown area that compromises the pre-amalgamation Toronto is where the elites reside. Many of them live in condos, have easy access to the subway, love riding their bicycles, and are often found on the left or far left of the political spectrum. They care about the environment, bike lanes, diversity, and if they have any objection to higher property and other taxes, they do not readily show it.

The suburbs are where the less beautiful people live. Many are immigrants who are forced to use their cars or spend hours taking public transportation because they do not have easy access to subways. Depending on where they live, they have to take two or three buses to reach a subway to head downtown. A lot of these residents are lower income people who worry more about whether they can afford to stay in their homes if taxes are increased than they do about saving the world from global warming. The differences between the suburbs and the downtown core played a prominent role in the election of Ford as Toronto's 64th mayor.

After Ford registered to run, the downtown elites, including Smitherman, didn't think Ford had any chance of success, As a result, the former cabinet minister did not spend any time attacking the Etobicoke councillor. That was until the next month when a poll came out showing Ford a close second to Smitherman. As anyone could have predicted, Pantalone was running a distant third.

In many ways, Ford more resembled one of the fringe candidates than he did a mainstream experienced councillor who had a legitimate shot. And given the low requirements for the mayoral race, there is never any shortage of these fringe candidates.

Many of fringe candidates that run municipally are single issue candidates. Someone with $200 can decide Toronto would be a much better place to live in if petunias were planted throughout the city. Although that candidate has no possibility of ending up as mayor, there is no doubt that if he or she did win, the city would be overrun with flowers.

Ford ran on the mantras of "stopping the gravy train" and "respect for taxpayers." Unlike candidates who promise to do things they have no intention of carrying through with, no one doubted what Ford would at least try to do if elected. He kept his message simple. And unlike the fringe candidates, the future mayor's message resonated with a lot of Torontonians. Although he did have positions on other issues, he was able to stick to his message of respect for taxpayers and stopping the gravy train.

Ford promised once elected he would scrap the Land Transfer Tax and the Vehicle Registration Tax, the taxes that played a large part in Miller's and the left's downfall. He also promised to hold the line on property taxes. He further promised to scrap the proposed light rail system for subways and "subways, subways, subways" was added to his slogans of respect for taxpayers and stopping the gravy train. Ford also wanted to contract out some city services like garbage collection and make the Toronto Transit Commission (TTC) an essential service. Although this would be more expensive, transit strikes could never again put the city at a standstill until the unions were ordered back to work by the legislature after millions of dollars were lost to Toronto businesses.

As far as seats in the Ontario Legislature and the federal House of Commons, Toronto has 22 ridings, each with an elected Ontario MPP and federal MP. Each of these same areas have two city councillors for a total of 44. Ford promised if he could, he would reduce the size of local government to half the number of present councillors and thereby reduce the size of the municipal government.

People understood there was no way this would ever come to pass. The Ontario government would be the one to make the change and would only do so if the city agreed. The thought of most councillors voting themselves out of jobs was impossible to comprehend but people had no doubt if a Mayor Ford could do it, he would.

When Smitherman realized Ford was his main competition, he focused his attacks on the Ward 2 councillor. Smitherman, who had been the first openly gay cabinet minister in the province, attacked the mayor about his previous comments on AIDS. Ford ignored the question and countered he would never waste a billion of taxpayers' dollars the way his opponent did with eHealth. Ford supporters and the undecided who thought their tax money was wasted by all levels of government, loved it despite the politically incorrect comment Ford had earlier made. When Ford's behaviour and statements became an issue, the councillor would counter with how Smitherman and the Liberals wasted money.

Another scandal involving Ford and alcohol emerged during the campaign. The *Toronto Sun* dug up records that showed the mayoral candidate was arrested in 1999 in Florida where he was vacationing with his girlfriend Renata who he married the following year.

The documentation showed Ford was arrested and charged with driving under the influence (DUI) and with possession of marijuana after arresting officers discovered a joint in his pocket. He later pleaded guilty to the DUI and was fined. The marijuana charge was dropped and he was prohibited from driving in the state of Florida for one year.

When Ford was confronted with this incident, he denied being charged with possession of marijuana. He later said he had forgotten about it because he was so concerned with the charge of failing to provide breath samples. But the Florida records clearly show he was charged with, and pleaded guilty to, a DUI not to failing to provide breath samples. This was another example of Ford lying to attempt to conceal an embarrassing fact.

While supporters of Smitherman and other candidates were overjoyed with this, the first poll taken after the revelation showed the Etobicoke councillor on the rise. Fiscal conservatism trumped what he did or didn't do 11 years earlier.

After the election the Smitherman team admitted voters had a somewhat difficult time understanding where their candidate stood. His years with the Ontario Liberals clearly marked him as a progressive. Although he began the campaign more to the centre to differentiate himself from Miller, he then tried to move to the right when it became obvious Ford was doing well in the polls. Of course even moving to the right he was no match for the candidate obsessed with governments wasting other peoples' money. Smitherman's place on the political spectrum was wherever he thought it was beneficial to be at the time.

When the results were tabulated for the election held on October 25, 2010, Ford won with 47% of the vote. Ford obtained 383, 501 votes, a healthy margin over Smitherman's 289, 832. As always expected, Pantalone, finished third garnering 95,482 votes. Rocco Rossi who had dropped out of the race but whose name remained on the ballot ended up a distant fourth with 5,012 votes. Not only David Miller but the Miller-style of government was over, at least for the next four years.

Not surprisingly, the vote ended up being split geographically. Smitherman did well in the old city of Toronto while Ford was extremely popular in the suburbs.

The reaction of the left to Ford's win bordered on the absurd. Toronto has a weak mayoral system where the mayor is essentially only one vote on the 45-member council. Those who predicted the demise of the city if the politically incorrect Ford won, were now saying it was no big deal; after all he was only one vote on council. It would not be long before these same people who crowed the mayor had only one vote were back to saying the new mayor would ultimately destroy life as we know it in Toronto. The city was doomed!

Chapter 3

Mayor Rob Ford, 2010 – 2014

Long term Councillor Kyle Rae who decided not to seek re-election in 2010 predicted Ford would not get anything done because he did only have one vote and his proposals would be blocked by the majority on council who were on the left. Rae, who had become a poster boy for the excessive spending at city hall by throwing himself a retirement party costing the taxpayers $12,000, was not far off the mark in his prediction of the difficulties the prudent Ford would have in getting his agenda through. Many of the councillors were more interested in stopping Ford than stopping the gravy train that so many Toronto voters cast their ballots for.

Ford was sworn in on December 7, 2010. The mayor elect needed someone to put the chain of office around his neck and make a short speech. Unlike his predecessors who chose politicians, judges or highly respected Toronto citizens to do the honour, Ford chose Don Cherry.

Cherry, a former hockey player, NHL coach and commentator on Hockey Night in Canada's *Coach's Corner*, is probably one of the few people who is not only further to the right than Ford but who is more politically incorrect than the incoming mayor. And he doesn't even live in Toronto.

Cherry, who always dresses in high-collared shirts, outlandish sports jackets and ties, wore pink for the occasion. During his speech he said he was wearing pink as a tribute to all the pinkos out there who like bicycles and everything. Cherry, who lives in Mississauga just outside Toronto, said

Ford would be the best mayor the city ever had and the "left-wing kooks" could put that in their pipes and smoke it. As commentators have pointed out, Cherry's speech was insulting to all those Torontonians who do not share the political views of Cherry and Ford. Cherry's appearance and speech was an unusual beginning to what would become a most unusual four year term of the new council.

Nevertheless, Ford got off to a relatively good start during his honeymoon period. Although criticized for leaving out downtown left wing councillors from important positions such as the mayor's executive committee, he really did not act any differently than mayors who preceded him. A suburban councillor like Ford would never have been chosen to be on Miller's executive committee. These appointments go to people who the mayor believes will help implement his or her agenda.

At the beginning of 2011, Ford was able to get some of his proposals and promises through council. The council did away with the hated vehicle registration tax that saw residents of the city pay $60 to register their vehicles in addition to what they are also required to pay the province. Council also passed Ford's promise to make the TTC an essential service. In addition to doing away with the millions of dollars in lost business when the transit system is shut down, the traffic, congested at the best of times, makes it almost impossible for people to get to work and attend to the things they have to do.

Since first being elected to council in 2000, Ford had always railed against the councillors' office budgets. After becoming mayor, he was successful in reducing those budgets from $50,445 to $30,000 a year. This reduction however, would not last.

Another promise Ford made during the campaign was to save the city some money by contracting out some of the work done by municipal employees. In late 2011, council voted to privatize garbage collection west of Yonge Street that is acknowledged to be the dividing line between the eastern and western parts of the city. Proposals to provide this service were sent out and ultimately Green for Life Environmental East Corporation

(GFL) was awarded the contract. It was estimated the private garbage collection from 165,000 homes west of Yonge Street would save Toronto approximately $11 million a year. The privatization would also result in the reduction of about 300 highly paid unionized workers.

The first day of private collection saw the garbage either picked up late or not at all. To the union-loving, anti-capitalist left, that was all they needed to know to scream that privatization was a mistake. As predicted by the left, life as we knew it in at least the west end of the city was coming to an end. The union representing Toronto's outside workers set up a hotline in order that residents in the west part of Toronto who were upset could complain.

Management at GFL explained the initial problems were a result of the company's employees not being familiar with their routes. After the first day of collection, the pick-ups went smoothly. According to city staff, there were a few complaints as there always are regarding service providers but that GFL not only dealt with these complaints but did so in a reasonable time. Chalk up one for the taxpayers.

Despite Ford's promise to also scrap the city's land transfer tax, it was left in place. The city could just not afford to forgo that revenue.

Being on the right, Ford was seen as anti-union. During his term in office, with the exception of a one week strike by library workers, the mayor managed to keep labour peace, something his union-loving predecessor could not accomplish. Toronto residents were not faced with any strikes such as the 39-day strike that left garbage rotting throughout the hot summer that doomed Miller during his final term and prevented his fellow traveller Pantalone from having any realistic chance of becoming mayor in 2010. The guy who hated unions and wanted everything privatized managed to reach agreements with Toronto's major unions.

When their contracts ended, the city was able to reduce the workforce through buyouts and attrition and tightened the rules on so called "jobs for life" that saw workers with 10 years seniority offered jobs at similar pay if their positions were terminated or contracted out. Ending jobs for life was bound to save the taxpayers money in the future.

Council was also successful in making paramedics an essential service, preventing them from lawfully striking and risking the health and lives of Toronto residents.

In early 2011, council voted to spend $3 million on consultants to find savings in order to help Ford keep his promise of stopping the gravy train. After the first report was issued, it was clear that most of the city's spending was on core items that could not be abolished. Many of these expenditures were mandated by the province and could not be done away with without the consent of the Ontario government.

In what did not help the mayor's cause, after the report came out his brother Doug, the councillor for Ward 2, focused his attack on libraries. Doug told the media there were more libraries in his ward than there were Tim Hortons restaurants and he was prepared to have at least one in his riding close down to save the taxpayers money.

Writer Margaret Atwood got into the act on Twitter that created a backlash. It didn't help the cause of the Ford brothers after Doug said he wouldn't recognize Atwood if he passed her on the street. This incident reveals the combativeness of the Ford brothers that observers would see more of over the next four years.

For 2011, the first budget of the Ford administration, a balanced budget was obtained without any property tax increases. This was accomplished by dipping into the surplus and reserve funds. In 2012, after realizing many of the city's expenditures could not be cut, there were some cuts to services. One of the plus sides to revenue was from the overheated Toronto real estate market that yielded greater than anticipated land transfer tax revenues. Surplus revenues were used for the 2013 budget.

During the last four years of the Miller administration, residential property taxes increased by 3.8%, 3.75%, 4% and 2.9% respectively. During the first Ford budget in 2011, these taxes remained constant. There were tax increases in 2012, 2013 and 2014 of 2.5%, 2% and 2.71% respectively.

Along with stopping the gravy train and respect for taxpayers, another one of Ford's mantras was "subways, subways, subways." While others wanted to improve Toronto's transportation system with Light Rail Transit

(LRT) and put more buses on the congested streets, Ford wanted subways. Ford thought subways should be built in the suburbs and not basically confined to the downtown area where the beautiful people live.

Residents like to see Toronto as a world class city but in comparison to many others, the transit system leaves a lot to be desired. The only new subway built in recent times was the Sheppard Avenue line. Constructed under Miller's predecessor, Mel Lastman, it is often referred to as the subway to nowhere. It goes a short distance on Sheppard Avenue to Don Mills Road and then ends rather abruptly.

The downtown area or the old city of Toronto is well served by subways. No one is too far away from the main north-south trains or the east-west line. But for those who live in the outer reaches of Scarborough, North York and Etobicoke, people dependent upon public transit often have to take more than one bus to reach a subway line if they are travelling downtown. People in these areas, unlike the perceived latte-sipping beautiful people who live downtown and prefer to ride bikes and take the handy subways, many suburbanites are blue collar and low income people or recent immigrants to Canada. Many are Ford supporters who feel they have just as much right to subways as the downtowners do.

One of Ford's promises was to end the "war against the car." Real or imagined, the Miller administration seemed more concerned with building bike lanes and championing light rail at the expense of reducing traffic on the heavily congested streets. Unless someone in the 'burbs wants to spend hours on public transportation, they have no alternative but to drive. And congestion in the downtown core is right up there with the worst cities in North America.

Transit City came into existence in 2007. A joint venture between the city and the Toronto Transit Commission, the agency's initial plans called for the construction of seven light rail lines in Toronto, most of them on major city thoroughfares. The light rail trains would be completely separated from vehicle traffic. The tracks would take up room on the street, something Ford and his supporters saw as aiding the war against the car.

During Miller's term, St. Clair Avenue, a major east-west street, was rejigged to provide a separate right of way for streetcars. During construction, businesses on the street suffered, some going out of business and the normal traffic congestion grew worse. After completion there were less parking spaces available and many people who would patronize stores on St. Clair went out of their way to avoid the street. Ford did not want other streets such as Sheppard, Eglinton and Finch to end up the same way.

Some of the spending on the proposed LRT lines was going to be paid for by the provincial and federal governments. Shortly after the 2010 municipal election, Ford announced Transit City was dead; he wanted subways, subways, subways.

The new mayor got some but not all of what he wanted. Construction had already been started on the Sheppard LRT and two thirds of the money for the project came from the federal and provincial governments. The city was told if construction on that line was halted, Toronto and not the other levels of governments would have to foot the bill for the costs of cancellation.

After negotiations were held, Transit City's money was put into the Eglinton LRT with much of the line running underground. The Sheppard construction is also continuing even though the LRT has been cancelled.

The Bloor-Danforth subway line will be extended from Kennedy Station in the east to McCowan, getting rid of the light rail line currently connected to Kennedy. What other subways or light rail will be built in the future became a major issue during the 2014 campaign.

Nothing much of note occurred during the first half of 2013 other than the scandals that enveloped the mayor, most notably the revelation that a cellphone video existed that showed His Worship smoking what appeared to be crack cocaine.

Chapter 4

Crack and other scandals

If there was ever a politician who was subjected to as much scrutiny by the media as Robert Bruce Ford was, it is hard to know who that person is. Although the *Toronto Star* once endorsed Ford for councillor when he first ran in Etobicoke's Ward 2, the newspaper became his most vociferous critic. But the *Star* was not alone.

The leftist elites in the city, including most of the mainstream media couldn't stand the mayor. He was a conservative, always railing against the pet projects of special interest groups in favour of the overtaxed residents of Toronto. And when the crack scandal emerged, even the so called populist *Toronto Sun* turned against Ford.

On top of that, Ford was loud, sometimes obnoxious, and was generally characterized by his political enemies as a buffoon. Ford was prone to use unparliamentary language when describing councillors and often used politically incorrect language such as the time he said Orientals work like dogs and showed no apparent sympathy for AIDS victims. The longer he remained in the public eye, the more the media went after him. An example of the viciousness of the media occurred when Ford was running for mayor in 2010. An article written by Stephen Marche and published in the *Globe and Mail* shortly before Election Day, used the word "fat" 17 times to describe the 300 plus pound candidate. The article contained such brilliant lines as "His angry fat is perfectly of our time," and "The mounds of fat that encircle Rob Ford's body like great deflated tires of the defeated are truly unprecedented in Canadian politics."

Marche obviously never saw former Liberal MP Elinor Caplan waddle into the House of Commons. The *Globe* would never point that out because she was a liberal and a Liberal. She was one of them.

Although some people wonder how that article got past the editors, no doubt they were laughing at Ford along with Marche. The newspaper later pulled the column from its website after it became the subject of a lot of social media discussion.

There are many people in Toronto who not only do not support Ford but actually hate him. It is the same derangement syndrome that the caring and compassionate American left had for George W. Bush. Ford became a large target in the age of YouTube where everyone has a cellphone camera. And there was no incident too small that would be uploaded to YouTube and then gleefully reported by the mainstream media in order to make fun of Toronto's mayor.

On one occasion, Ford announced publicly he was going to lose weight. In 2012, he took part in the "Cut the Waist Challenge" wherein he vowed to lose 50 pounds in six months. He was to weigh in once a week so the public would know how his diet was going.

Well someone recorded a video of the mayor leaving a KFC location carrying a bag of food. The media had a field day with it, laughing about how the mayor was trying to lose weight by eating fried chicken. In the end, he gained a little weight. The media no doubt considered this a "weighty" issue, pardon the pun.

While limousines for the use of councillors was ended during the Miller administration, one was always at the disposal of the mayor. Very few people begrudged the fact the chief magistrate of Canada's largest city, the fourth largest city in North America, had the use of a limo. But Ford eschewed not only the use of the limousine but until the latter stages of his term, refused to have a driver. The mayor preferred to drive his own Cadillac Escalade around the city.

On one occasion, a picture of Ford was taken driving on the Gardiner Expressway while talking on a hand-held cellphone, an offence under the province's *Highway Traffic Act*. While he was definitely in the wrong, the media made a big deal out of it. Ford was forced to apologize.

Ford has been the constant subject of complaints to the integrity commissioner and other bodies as well as the defendant in civil suits both threatened and commenced. While most of these complaints were resolved in the mayor's favour, the media and the Ford-haters were not happy someone like Ford was in office and subjected him to a variety of complaints. He had to be done away with at any cost.

While the 2010 municipal campaign was winding down, city council granted a 21-year lease extension to Tuggs Incorporated that operated what was then the Boardwalk Café on the Toronto waterfront. Contrary to the recommendation of city staff, the lease was approved without requesting competitive bids. This sole source lease granted to Tuggs' owner, George Foulidis, caused a lot of controversy especially in the ward the restaurant was located it. The lease to Tuggs was another reason incumbent Sandra Bussin was trounced by newcomer Mary-Margaret McMahon. While there were other factors that angered voters about Bussin, including her council spending, the sole sourced lease granted to Tuggs on terms favourable to the corporation played a not insignificant role in Bussin's large defeat at the hands of a candidate who had never before held elective office.

In July 2010, while being interviewed on *Newstalk1010*, Ford said he thought someone must be getting money under the table but refused to say anything else because the information regarding the terms of the deal was confidential.

A few days later, the *Toronto Sun* wrote about Ford's remarks saying the mayoral candidate described the Tuggs deal as "corruption and skullduggery." The newspaper also claimed Ford suspected the sole source lease was pushed by Bussin because Foulidis had contributed to her campaigns over the years.

Foulidis demanded an apology from Ford and after none was forthcoming, he sued the mayor for libel, claiming $6 million in damages. The lawsuit was later thrown out. Besides not being sure Foulidis was the chief officer of Tuggs, the court ruled Ford's comments fell short of libel.

The *Toronto Sun* used much stronger language in describing what Ford said than the councillor and candidate for mayor actually used. Ford never used the word "corruption" in describing the lease with Tuggs. What was truly strange about this lawsuit was although Ford and another party were sued, Foulidis did not bother suing the *Toronto Sun* for libel despite the fact the newspaper used the much stronger language to describe the deal such as the word "corruption" than Ford did during his radio interview. Yet the *Sun* was never sued.

During the same month, candidate Ford threatened to sue the *Toronto Star* for libel after the newspaper wrote about how Ford was no longer allowed to coach football at Newtonbrook Secondary School after a 2001 incident in which he had a physical altercation with a student player. Ford denied he had an altercation and issued a libel notice. However, he did not pursue the claim.

The *Toronto Star* filed a complaint with the integrity commissioner after Ford announced he would no longer speak with the newspaper or provide information that was routinely sent to other media organizations. Later the integrity commissioner ruled Ford did not breach the city's code of conduct and wondered whether it was even possible for a corporation like Torstar that owns the newspaper to make a complaint to the integrity commissioner.

During May 2011, a request was made for an audit of Ford's 2010 campaign spending, claiming he may have spent more than he was legally entitled to do and that he may have illegally borrowed money for his campaign from a company. The city's Compliance Audit Committee agreed to the audit, but the mayor went to court in an attempt to reverse the decision. Prior to a judicial determination being made, Ford dropped his appeal and agreed to an audit. The audit found there were spending irregularities but the Compliance Audit Committee then refused to appoint a special prosecutor or recommend the mayor face charges. After all that, Ford was in the clear concerning his expenses.

In July 2011, a complaint was made that Ford failed to report all his spending after his office expenses appeared to be low. Not only was this complaint dismissed but once again having a Ford-hating leftist complain about a politician not spending enough of the taxpayers' money only endeared the mayor to members of Ford Nation, his loyal citizen support group.

In April 2012, Toronto's Chief Medical Officer of Health, Dr. David McKeown, said he would recommend to the city's board of health that speed limits across Toronto be lowered in order to save lives. Ford, who had always battled against the left's "war against the car," said McKeown's idea was "nuts" and said his salary of $290,000 a year was "ridiculous." Brother Doug got into the act and wondered aloud why McKeown even had a job.

McKeown made a complaint to the integrity commissioner who reported both brothers had violated Toronto's code of conduct. Before any further action could be taken, Rob and Doug apologized to the doctor. Again, the brothers' remarks about a city official should not have been made by a mayor and a councillor but a lot of Torontonians totally agreed with what they said.

In September 2012, complaints were again made to the integrity commission alleging the mayor had his staff help with his duties as a high school football coach and by so doing, he was improperly using city resources for non-city business. This complaint was dismissed by the integrity commissioner. Ford got absolutely no credit for giving up his time to coach football at Don Bosco, an area where many of the students are from lower income families and football can be an alternative to joining a gang.

In September 2012, Toronto's Ombudsman, Fiona Crean, began an investigation into the accusation that Ford was manipulating the selection of citizens appointed to fill various city boards and agencies. Crean later issued a report finding this was happening but her report was criticized by some councillors mainly because there was no written evidence of interference with the selection process. Despite these weaknesses, the city changed how it appoints citizens to municipal boards and agencies in an attempt to prevent interference in the future. Nothing happened to the mayor as a result of the ombudsman's report.

In October 2013, Councillor Paul Ainslie voted against the proposed Scarborough subway and in favour of light rail. What set Ainslie apart from other councillors who favoured light rail transit was that he represented a ward in Scarborough and his constituents would benefit the most by such a subway. Ford's response was to send out robocalls to Ainslie's constituents telling them what their councillor was doing. The Scarborough councillor then filed a complaint with the integrity commissioner. That complaint was not resolved at the time the 2014 campaign got underway.

It seemed the beleaguered mayor, when not under police surveillance, was always having to defend his actions before one city official or another.

Then there were also scandals in his personal life. The media reported police had attended the mayor's home on more than one occasion in relation to complaints about domestic violence. With the exception of an incident in 2008, charges were not laid.

In March of 2008, Ford called 911 after an incident between the councillor and his wife. According to Ford, his wife Renata was leaving the home and threatened to take his two children away. The following day Ford was charged with assault and uttering threats. Two months later the Crown withdrew both charges. According to prosecutors, there was no reasonable possibility of obtaining convictions due to credibility issues with Renata. Both Toronto police and prosecutors said she had given two different versions of the events and would be an unreliable witness.

Although the fact he had substance abuse problems did not fully reach the public until reports surfaced about the crack video in May, 2013, it was known the mayor was no stranger to alcohol. There was the incident at the Air Canada Centre when he was a councillor and then the revelation during the 2010 campaign that he had been convicted of DUI in Florida in 1999. Ford was criticized in the media for having his staff go to the liquor store to purchase his booze. Like driving his own car and picking up his own chicken, Ford used to purchase his own alcohol. But if he was seen leaving a liquor store, someone would snap a picture, upload it to the Internet and the media would make fun of Ford doing what thousands of other people do every day. It was only after this happened did the mayor get his staff to get liquor for him. It was hardly a spending scandal but it was big news for the left wing media.

When it was revealed that Deputy Mayor Norm Kelly, who took over the powers council later took away from Ford, had a party at his house and had gotten members of his staff to bring the beer, it was apparently no big deal.

The scrutiny Ford was put under would have been justified if other elected politicians were subjected to the same kind of close examination Ford was under. Having staff purchase alcohol was a big deal in an attempt to discredit Ford but not others such as Kelly.

Although the initial allegation of a video purporting to show Ford smoking what appeared to be crack cocaine and being drunk and hurling racial slurs caught the attention of the world, there was a much more serious scandal that saw a judge order the mayor removed from office. The mayor appealed the decision and it was reversed. Despite all of the scandals, some involving the use of illegal drugs, this was the closest Ford came to actually being removed from office.

The incident began while Ford was still a councillor. In 2008, the councillor set up the Rob Ford Football Foundation. The purpose of the non-profit was to raise money to allow disadvantaged youth to be able to play football, a sport Ford loves. The money would help the type of youth that attended Don Bosco Secondary School in Etobicoke where Ford was coaching. According to Ford, the money would be used to buy uniforms at a cost of approximately $400 per player.

Ford, using his city council letterhead sent fundraising letters to city lobbyists and raised $3,150 in that manner. After what he did became known, a complaint was made to Toronto's integrity commissioner.

Prior to the 2010 election, Janet Leiper, who was then the integrity commissioner, ruled Ford acted improperly and ordered him to return the money to the lobbyists. Council later voted to uphold Leiper's decision.

Ford refused to pay the money back. In February 2012 another motion was put before council to reverse the decision requiring the now mayor to reimburse the lobbyists for their donations to the football foundation. The motion easily passed. The majority of councillors saw the contributions as no big deal; the amount was small and Ford did not personally benefit from the funds solicited. All the money was to go to disadvantaged youth who just wanted to play football. This would normally have been a gesture the left love.

Ford spoke to the motion, making a passionate speech about his love of high school football and how being able to play kept some of the young men in school rather than dropping out and joining gangs. The mayor not only spoke to the motion but he voted on it. While it is arguable he had a right to speak and defend himself because he was on the hook to pay the $3,150, he ended up voting on a motion he had a personal interest in.

In March 2012, lawyer Clayton Ruby, a prominent Ford foe, announced he was commencing a lawsuit to have the mayor removed from office on the grounds he was in a conflict of interest when he voted, a breach of the provincial *Municipal Conflict of Interests Act*.

The named plaintiff was Paul Magder (not the well-known Toronto furrier of the same name) who seemed more concerned with getting rid of the mayor than whether or not any laws or rules were broken.

The matter was heard before Justice Charles Hackland of the province's Superior Court of Justice. On Nov. 26, 2012, Hackland ruled Ford had breached the Act. Under the draconian legislation, the justice had no alternative but to order the mayor removed from office. He could have ordered the mayor not to be eligible to run again for a specified period of time but declined to do so.

The only defences available to a municipal official who would otherwise be found to have been in conflict of interest and ordered removed from office are inadvertence or if an error in judgment was made in good faith. Inadvertence was never an issue; what Ford had done was deliberate. Hackland found from the evidence he heard that Ford never did attempt to familiarize himself with the conflict of interest rules and therefore his "error in judgment" was not made in good faith. The justice ordered the mayor removed from office.

Ford's lawyers immediately appealed to Divisional Court and obtained a stay allowing the mayor to remain in office until the disposition of the appeal.

On Jan. 25, 2013, Divisional Court released its decision. The three justices were unanimous in allowing the appeal and quashing Hackland's order. It was a decision Ford's critics were quick to call "a technicality."

While generally agreeing with Hackland's findings that there was a conflict of interest that was not inadvertent nor a good faith error, the justices had difficulty with the earlier motion adopted by city council.

After Leiper released her first report on the matter, council adopted her recommendations including the one requiring Ford to pay $3,150, money he had never personally received, to the lobbyists. When a member of a municipality is found to be in a conflict, the municipality can impose penalties that include a fine and repaying money improperly received back to the city. But Divisional Court ruled city council had no jurisdiction to order Ford to pay monies he never received to third parties, in this case, the lobbyists. The motion by council was found by the court to be a nullity. Since that motion was a nullity, the motion to overturn the decision that Ford pay the money, the one Ford was in a conflict of interest when he voted on it, was also ruled a nullity.

Ruby and Magder applied for leave to appeal this decision to the Supreme Court of Canada. The country's top court declined to hear the matter and as is their usual practice, did not give reasons for their decision. Ford was allowed to remain in office.

Coincidence or not, shortly after Ford was ordered removed from office and then reinstated, media reports emerged suggesting Toronto's chief magistrate might have a problem with alcohol that went beyond the couple of incidents of drinking and driving in Florida and being drunk at a hockey game.

The mayor attended a function in early March 2013. Also present was Sarah Thomson, the mayoral wannabe who has never held elected office but who ran for mayor in 2010 and 2014 before dropping out and throwing what little support she had to Smitherman in 2010 and John Tory in 2014.

Thomson said Ford made inappropriate comments to her, telling her he had just come back from Florida and she should have come with him because his wife was not there. When they posed for pictures, Thomson alleged the mayor placed his hand on her buttocks. Some in the media, in true media fashion, dubbed this "Assgate."

According to some people who were there, Thomson suggested a friend also named Sarah have her picture taken with Ford. Hopefully the mayor would grab her ass and someone would take a picture and Thomson could then use it in her planned run for mayor the following year.

Although Thomson discussed what happened while she was still at the event, she did not act like it was a big deal. It was reported she told a pay duty police officer about it as she was leaving the function. When the officer asked her if she wished to make a formal complaint, Thomson declined.

The alleged incident was made public by Thomson in the way it would be expected of children, teens and immature adults; she posted all about it on Facebook. Ignored since she dropped out during the 2010 campaign, the editor of *Women's Post* then got an additional 15 minutes of fame by giving media interviews about what happened. She said the mayor was "wasted" and thought it was as a result of using cocaine. She knew what to look for in people who are high on cocaine because she had Googled it.

Ford denied he was wasted or that he ever spoke to or touched Thomson inappropriately. Thomson had changed her version over the following days and a lot of people who were not supporters of the mayor and his platform of stopping the gravy train, were not rushing to believe her. To his political enemies, piling on Ford was a sport.

This incident would have been minor and able to be written off as an act by a political opponent wishing to gain an advantage were it not for one thing. The allegation that Ford was at least drunk and possibly had an alcohol problem, led the media in general and the *Toronto Star* in particular to investigate other possible incidents where the mayor had consumed alcohol to excess. And they found them. The *Star* got reporter Robyn Doolittle to investigate the Thomson incident and she then followed up other allegations about the mayor and his drinking.

On March 26, 2013, Doolittle and fellow *Toronto Star* reporter Kevin Donovan reported about the mayor's attendance at the annual Garrison Ball. This event took place just a few days before the alleged incident of Ford allegedly groping Thomson.

The Garrison Ball honours certain members of Canada's military and also raises money for the Wounded Warriors charity. High ranking military officials, Defense Minister Peter Mackay, as well as the who's who of Toronto Society were present at the event.

According to reports, Ford showed up late, accompanied by some others including Sandro Lisi whose name would later be linked to Ford's use of crack and the police investigation into the mayor.

Although some attendees told the *Star* they could not smell alcohol on the mayor's breath, other sources told the newspaper he appeared to be drunk, high on drugs or suffering from a medical condition. He was described as stumbling and rambling. According to some reports, he had almost fallen on the stairs.

Some sources confirmed Ford was asked to leave the event while others were said to have told the mayor's chief of staff, Mark Towhey, to get him out of there. The mayor left about an hour after he arrived and the circumstances of his leaving became a matter of some controversy.

It was around this time that members of Ford's inner circle were reported to have told him to go into rehab for his drinking problem or otherwise seek help.

In the article by Doolittle and Donovan about the Garrison Ball, reference to Ford's going to the Bier Market on St. Patrick's Day, 2012 was made. More details of Ford's activities on that day would come to light after information the police gathered, including interviews with some of the mayor's staff, were made public in November, 2013.

There is really not much need to go into great detail about the crack scandal. It was not only big news in Toronto and Canada but received a lot of attention around the world. US outlets like CNN that usually avoid anything short of mass murder north of the border sent reporters to Toronto as did other foreign media agencies. Ford became a laughing stock and was regularly poked fun at by late night comedians in the United States. Ford himself appeared on the *Jimmy Kimmel Show*. There are people in countries most people in North America never heard of that while not being able to find Canada on a map knew the name of the mayor of Toronto. It is probably not much of an exaggeration to say Rob Ford became the most famous municipal politician in the history of civilization.

On May 16, 2013 the US publication *Gawker* published an article reporting the mayor of Toronto was captured on video with a glass pipe in his hand and smoking what appeared to be crack cocaine. The same story appeared on the website of the *Toronto Star* a few hours later.

Although none of the media had a copy of the video, John Cook, then the editor-in-chief of *Gawker.com* had come to Toronto after being contacted by a drug dealer who offered it for sale for $100,000, Cook claimed to have seen it. Prior to the information going public, *Toronto Star* reporters Doolittle and Donovan also said they had seen a video of Rob Ford smoking what purported to be crack cocaine. They viewed this video on a cellphone while in a car with the person who was attempting to sell it.

At the time *Gawker* published their story, the *Star* was still deciding whether or not to purchase the video. Although they had decided not to spend $100,000, the paper was willing to purchase it for a few thousand dollars.

According to Doolittle, the person in the video exhibited the same mannerisms she noticed Ford had when she had covered him for the *Star*. And the reporter observed he was using a lighter to heat the bottom of the pipe suggesting it contained cocaine and not marijuana that would be lit at the top.

As a show of good faith, the person who had the video provided both *Gawker* and the *Toronto Star* with a still picture. Although there was some initial confusion, this picture was not a screenshot from the video but was taken at a completely different time. It showed Ford with three alleged drug dealers posing for the picture outside of an address in Etobicoke later identified by Toronto police as a crack den. One of the men posing for the picture, Anthony Smith, was shot to death prior to the picture being released. The other two were later arrested during the culmination of a police operation dubbed "Project Traveller."

A few days after news of the video broke, Ford made his first statement about the video. He said he does not smoke crack and is not a crack addict. It was noticed he did not say he had never smoked crack. Ford would later say the video did not exist and he could not comment on something that did not in fact exist.

Ford also blamed the *Toronto Star,* accusing Canada's largest circulation daily of making up the story about the crack video. While the *Toronto Star* had done its best to turn incidents whose newsworthiness were questionable into front page stories if they thought it could damage the mayor they hated, it was hard for many to believe the newspaper and two professional journalists would have fabricated the whole thing. Still there was no conclusive proof it was the mayor rather than a Ford lookalike. Nor was there proof of what if anything was in the pipe.

In a poll taken at the beginning of June, half of the respondents did not believe the video existed. While some people believed Cook, Doolittle and Donovan were lying outright and nothing existed, others questioned whether the person in the purported video was actually the mayor and wondered if drug dealers provided an altered video in order to extract cash from the media.

The dealers raised their price to $200,000 and *Gawker* set out to raise the funds through crowdsourcing. *Gawker* did in fact raise the money but then claimed the dealer who was to sell the video to them had disappeared and they lost contact with him. The money raised was later given to charities.

On June 13, about a month after the release of the existence of the crack video, police in Toronto and other areas in Ontario conducted a massive sweep as part of an ongoing investigation named "Project Traveller." Most of the arrests took place in the large subsidized housing project on

Dixon Road in Etobicoke. These buildings are close to 15 Windsor Road, the address later identified as the crack house where the still picture of Ford was taken.

The purpose of Project Traveller was to target a gang known as the Dixon City Blood. Police agencies were attempting to break up a sophisticated gun and drug operation.

That day police arrested 44 people who initially faced 224 charges. Among those arrested was the person who showed the video to Doolittle and Donovan as well as the two surviving men who were seen with Ford in the picture taken on Windsor Road.

After these arrests, Toronto Police Chief Bill Blair announced that Ford's name was mentioned in several of the telephone conversations that police had listened to and there were discussions about a video of the mayor using drugs. Toronto police had learned of the purported video before it was initially reported by *Gawker*. As a result, on May 18 the Toronto Police Service began a new operation known as "Project Brazen 2." This investigation, including wiretaps and surveillance, concentrated on the mayor and at least one of his known associates, Alexander (Sandro) Lisi, as well as others.

The wiretaps constituted evidence in criminal proceedings and as such could not be released to the media or the public. In order to obtain the legal right to intercept private communications, police had to apply for authorizations. This is done by filing what is known as an Information to Obtain Search Warrants or an ITO.

Lawyers for media outlets applied to the Ontario Superior Court requesting that the ITOs used in these operations be made public on the grounds that as it involved the mayor, it was in the public interest to release information that otherwise would remain sealed until such time as it was used as evidence in a criminal proceeding. Justice Ian Nordheimer would later order some portions of the ITOs released.

October 2013 was not a good month for Mr. Lisi. At the beginning of the month he and another person, an Etobicoke dry cleaner, were arrested. Lisi, who had a record for assaults and making threats was charged with trafficking in marijuana, possession of marijuana, possession of property obtained by crime and conspiracy to commit an indictable offence. He was released on bail and Ford told the media he was very surprised at the arrest of his friend.

At the end of the month, Lisi was again arrested and released on bail. This time he was charged at with one count of extortion. It was alleged he extorted a drug dealer in order to recover the video of Ford smoking crack cocaine.

The end of October saw Justice Nordheimer order the first batch of information contained in the ITOs released to the public. Although Ford was not, and still has not been charged with any criminal offence, the release of the documents as well as videos and pictures resulted in a marked change in the crack scandal.

Ordered the day before, the information was made public on the morning of October 31 and later that day, Toronto Police Chief Bill Blair held a press conference. Blair confirmed that a video purporting to show the mayor of Toronto seemingly smoking crack did in fact exist. According to the chief, the video was deleted but recovered from a hard drive that was seized during the Project Traveller raids. Responding to questions from reporters, Blair said he had personally seen it. When asked to comment on it, the chief said it was consistent with what had been reported in the media. Blair also described what he saw as "disappointing."

The release of the partially redacted ITOs showed Lisi had been under surveillance since the summer. Both he and Ford seemed to know they were being watched and Lisi was reported to have taken counter-surveillance measures. The fact that the mayor was under surveillance was not kept a secret. An aircraft was used that led to Ford and his neighbours to complain about the plane that seemed to always be flying over their homes.

Pictures were released showing some of the meetings between the mayor and Lisi. On one occasion, Ford showed up at a gas station. While he went into the convenience store to make a purchase, Lisi placed an envelope in the mayor's Escalade. The two spoke for a short time and then left separately.

In another observation, both men were seen to go into a park. After they left, police went in and found empty vodka and juice bottles.

Despite the suspicious activity, Ford was never charged with a criminal offense. Police stated since both Ford and Lisi seemed to know they were being watched, police never knew if the envelopes and packages they exchanged contained illegal substances or were in fact attempts by Ford and Lisi to be stopped and possibly arrested by police for exchanging envelopes that did not contain anything illegal.

While Lisi was charged with extortion after it was alleged he tried to extort drug dealers to recover the video, none of his drug charges involved Ford. And Ford himself was never charged with any crime despite the hours of being tracked by police.

Initially after the release of the ITOs, Ford refused to comment saying he would like to but could not since the matter was before the courts. This seemed a strange thing to say considering the fact he was not facing any criminal charges.

Ford's brother Doug went on the attack, saying Chief Blair was politically motivated in going after his brother. This would not be the only time Ford's older brother would go after Blair.

Blair was criticized in some circles for conducting Project Brazen 2, the operation centering on Ford and Lisi. While the chief is a sworn police officer, he is also a politician whose job it is to negotiate the police budget with city council. Acting in this capacity while his officers conducted an operation to see if the mayor was involved in criminal activity was seen by many to be a conflict of interest. While Blair denied there was a conflict, he eventually handed the investigation over to the Ontario Provincial Police (OPP).

Any use of drugs by Ford, either in videos or still photographs, was insufficient lay drug charges against Toronto's chief magistrate. In order to obtain a conviction, prosecutors must prove beyond a reasonable doubt the substance was in fact an illegal narcotic. Short of actually catching the mayor in possession of illegal drugs that could be properly analyzed which never happened, he could not be charged.

No doubt what the Toronto police were hoping for was to get evidence that Ford had taken part in the alleged extortion of the drug dealers together with Lisi in an attempt to obtain the crack video. In what was somewhat underplayed by the mainstream media, the OPP found no evidence of Ford being guilty of extortion. In fact the OPP determined if Ford had anything to do with extortion he was probably the victim of the drug dealers that wanted payment in exchange for handing over the incriminating video. They found no evidence that could lead to charges against the mayor. Toronto police, obviously disappointed, said Project Brazen 2 was still ongoing.

The release of the ITOs marked a significant event in Ford's term as mayor. Councillors who were previously friendly to the mayor and sympathized with any possible substance abuse problems joined the others who were calling on him to resign or at a minimum, take a leave of absence and get some help. The more conservative media such as the *National Post* and *Toronto Sun* also joined on calls for him to resign. Ford may not have united the city but he managed to unite the mainstream media.

The release of the ITOs added significant details to what transpired on St. Patrick's Day, 2012, the day the mayor ventured out to Bier Market. The additional information came from police interviews with members of Ford's staff who had firsthand information about that day. Former staffers would provide more information to the media.

According to these sources, one of the women visiting the mayor that evening was a paid escort. After he was prevented from smoking hash at city hall, Ford and others took a cab to a pub on Church Street. It is alleged Ford called the taxi driver a "Paki" and mocked his accent.

Around midnight, Ford still wanted to party and the group went to the Bier Market where he and those who accompanied him were put into a private room. This is when a waiter claims he saw Ford and a woman doing a line of cocaine. But there were various accounts of whether or not the mayor was inebriated, doing drugs and whether he left on his own accord or was kicked out. The group later returned to city hall where it was alleged the mayor got into a physical altercation with male staffers and called three women staffers, "liberal bitches."

At that time, it was alleged Ford claimed he had had sex with a former staffer and told her, "I'm going to eat you out" and "I banged your pussy."

Ford denied all the allegations made against him that evening and blamed the *Toronto Star* that initially reported these facts as making it up because they were out to get him.

City council passed a motion requesting Ford take a leave of absence to get help. The motion was non-binding and Ford ignored it. The premier of Ontario held a press conference to announce the province would be willing to assist the city if council was unable to function. Premier Wynne also said she would be consulting with the two opposition parties hoping to get their consent so the provincial government could act quickly if it came down to having to intervene in the governing of Toronto. In the end, the province never did get involved. Despite the fact councillors spent a lot of time bemoaning what was happening, it was clear the city was still able to function.

The following day, Ford held a press conference. One unusual aspect to this meeting was that his wife Renata, who is almost never seen in public at mayoral events, was at his side.

At the conference, Ford denied he had used cocaine or consorted with prostitutes. He said a friend, Alana, was with him that St. Patrick's Day evening and resented the fact she was referred to as an escort. The mayor also said he would sue former members of his staff who were coming out with all these lies.

In what would shock the assembled members of the media as well as Torontonians and what was to become repeated constantly on US late night television shows, the mayor denied he ever told a female staffer "I want to eat your pussy." Ford said, "I'm happily married, I have more than enough to eat at home." The phrase "more than enough to eat at home" became a standard punch line that helped define Ford's term as mayor.

During this press conference Ford admitted he was then under the care of medical professionals although he would not provide details of who they were and what he was being treated for.

A few days into November, Ford admitted he did smoke crack cocaine about a year before when he was in one of his "drunken stupors." He said he was embarrassed about what he did in the past but the past cannot be changed. The mayor apologized to the residents of the city. Once again, Ford admitted lying because he was embarrassed.

After this revelation, the mayor quickly called another press conference that spawned speculation he was going to announce his resignation. But those who knew the mayor or had been following his career closely since 2000, doubted this would happen. When Ford spoke, he stated he would not resign but promised the mistakes he made would never, ever happen again. And again, he issued an apology. It was not the announcement of his resignation or his taking a leave of absence that many thought he would make.

Under Canada's constitution municipalities have no inherent jurisdiction; they only have the powers that are delegated to them by the province. It is provincial legislation that dictates the circumstances when an elected municipal official can be removed from office or prohibited from running for election. As far as criminal conduct is concerned, Ford could not be disqualified and thrown off city council unless he was actually in jail. Admitting to having engaged in criminal behaviour was not sufficient. Even had he been charged and convicted of a serious offence, he could still occupy his office unless and until he would be taken to jail and the steel doors slammed shut. There was no way under the circumstances Ford could be removed from office. Unlike jurisdictions such as British Columbia, Ontario does not have recall legislation. There was nothing the public could do.

After Ford admitted using crack cocaine but refused to step down, council began working on a motion to strip as many powers from the mayor as they legally could. For example, under Ontario law, only a mayor can declare a state of emergency. Although this and other designated powers could only have been taken away from Ford by the province, Premier Wynne said she would watch what was happening but would not act unless she absolutely had to.

Other powers the mayor of Toronto has such as the power to make appointments to committees were provided by council. Any powers not given by the province but given to the mayor by council could be taken away by council.

On November 18, council voted overwhelmingly to take away the powers of the mayor they legally could and gave them to Deputy Mayor Norm Kelly. Ford called the move a coup and likened council's actions to Saddam Hussein's invasion of Kuwait. It was even clearer at this time Ford was not going anywhere.

On December 4, 2013, more police wiretaps from Project Brazen 2 were released to the public. While none of these taps were of Ford speaking, there were more allegations made about the mayor. In an intercepted conversation between two drug dealers, one is heard telling the other he has photographs of Ford smoking not crack but heroin. The tapes indicated the mayor had visited 15 Windsor Road on April 20, 2013. This was the home in front of which the still picture of Ford posing with unsavoury characters had been taken. An intercepted call on that date revealed someone had asked another party to bring some drugs over to the house because Ford wanted them. Contrary to Ford's denials, the wiretaps revealed the house on Windsor Road was indeed a place where drugs were sold.

There was another conversation where a drug dealer indicated he had a picture of the mayor smoking rocks and was considering posting the photo on Instagram.

There were also discussions about Anthony Smith, the gangbanger who had posed with Ford in front of 15 Windsor Road and who was later gunned down. There were indications the infamous crack video had been on Smith's phone. While telephone conversations indicated the motive for Smith's killing was robbery, there were some in Ford's circle who were concerned Smith was murdered because he had the crack video. Toronto police later discounted any connection between Smith's death and the mayor.

The evidence showed when Ford went to Windsor Road on April 20, he had either lost his cellphone or it was stolen. A conversation between Lisi and a drug dealer had Lisi say if Ford's phone was not returned, the mayor would have "the heat" put on Dixon, meaning the criminal elements in the area. The gangsters became angered at this because they felt they had the upper hand; they had pictures and videos of Ford using illegal substances.

The evidence also revealed the drug dealer who had shown the video to Doolittle and Donovan received a call from a man he believed to be Ford. He said he was offered $5,000 and a car in exchange for the video. If true, this obviously wasn't enough. The dealer, Mohamed Sayid, was going for more. He tried to obtain $200,000 from *Gawker* and $100,000 from the *Toronto Star* in exchange for the video.

The police also had evidence that Ford was abusing alcohol. Ford denied he had a drinking problem although admitting he drank socially and said he may have driven while under the influence.

While there were a lot of statements of wrongdoing by the mayor on these released wiretaps, none of the intercepts contained evidence that could be used against Ford in a prosecution for a criminal offence. And it appears none of Ford's phone calls were intercepted by police and released to the public. But the release of this information only made the cries for Ford's resignation become louder.

There were other incidents as well that would have been considered relatively minor had they not involved Ford. Multicultural Toronto is home to various ethnic festivals during the summer when portions of major streets are blocked off. One of the oldest of these is the Taste of the Danforth. Begun in the early 1990s with very few attendees it has grown to host about 1.5 million people over a three-day period. A section of Danforth Avenue in the area known as Greektown is closed to traffic and visitors can avail themselves of entertainment and food provided by the areas many restaurants and businesses, most of them Greek.

In August 2013, Ford attended Taste of the Danforth. Apparently he was to meet some of his staff who would accompany him to the venue, but there was a miscommunication and the mayor went alone. Various videos were shot as well as selfies that showed Ford appearing to be inebriated and slurring his words. While some Torontonians wanted to discuss municipal issues with him, Ford announced he wanted to party and only wanted to talk about fun things.

Ford's Escalade was seen parked on nearby Greenwood Avenue, confirming he had driven to the event. Eventually some members of his staff showed up and he was later driven home. Ford admitted he had "a couple of beers" at the event but there was speculation he drank before driving to the festival. The videos and selfies of course were reported by the mainstream media and there were more calls from councillors and others for him to resign or at least take a leave of absence to seek treatment for substance abuse.

The year ended with *Toronto Star* reporter Daniel Dale issuing a libel notice against the mayor. An incident occurred in May 2012, when Dale was outside of the mayor's home in the early evening. Dale's explanation was he was looking at some vacant city land adjacent to Ford's home that the mayor wanted to purchase. Ford came out of his house and accused him of taking pictures of his home and his family. After police were called and examined the reporter's cellphone, no pictures could be found. This was consistent with Dale's denial of taking pictures of the house or Ford's children.

On December 9, 2013, *Vision TV* aired an interview of Ford by Conrad Black on the network's show, *The Zoomer*. During the interview Ford mentioned the Dale incident and said the reporter was in his backyard taking pictures. Dale had always denied he was on Ford's property. Ford then added that "I have little kids. When a guy's taking pictures of little kids, I don't want to say the word, but you start thinking, you know, what's this guy all about?"

Although Ford specifically refrained from calling the reporter a pedophile, Dale's position that was that the mayor's statement strongly implied he was one. The Notice of Libel named the mayor, *Vision TV* and Black.

The matter was resolved a few days later when Ford apologized and the libel action was not proceeded with. A couple of weeks later, the year that saw the mayor of Toronto go from a usual albeit controversial municipal official to a celebrity who was the subject of international media attention including the object of many US TV late night comedians, was over. Many people seemed shocked that Ford, although stripped of many of his powers, was still the mayor of Canada's largest city.

Chapter 5

The 2014 Toronto Election Campaign

Other than those Torontonians who could not believe Ford had not re-signed after having admitted smoking crack during one of his drunken stupors, no one was really surprised at what happened on January 2, 2014. On that day, the official 2014 municipal campaign began and Ford was at city hall bright and early in the morning to put his $200 down and formally register to run for a second term. With the media in tow, the mayor became the first candidate to register for the 2014 mayoral race.

By the time official nominations closed in September, there were over 70 people registered to run for the position of chief magistrate of the city of Toronto. The vast majority were candidates no one outside of their families and close friends ever heard of and had absolutely no chance of even coming close. For many of those marginal candidates why they decided to run for mayor, other than for their egos, remains a mystery.

It is the media who decides who the major candidates will be. These are the ones that are invited to the numerous (over 65 this year) debates and who receive publicity given to serious candidates. As the campaign went on, there were five main candidates. Besides Ford, the others were former Toronto school board trustee, councillor and NDP MP Olivia Chow, John Tory, former leader of the Progressive Conservative Party of Ontario, Karen Stintz and David Soknacki. Stintz was then a current councillor and Soknacki had previously represented a Scarborough ward as councillor. Soknacki also served as the city's budget chief under Miller during his first term.

September. 12 was the deadline when nominations closed. Any candidate who had not formally withdrawn from the race by that date had their name remain on the ballot for the October 27 election.

Stintz and Soknacki both dropped out before nominations closed. If the support for both these candidates were combined, they did not reach double digits.

Not surprisingly, Sarah Thomson who had been a major candidate in 2010, also ran but was by and large ignored. The media needed a major candidate who was a woman and that role was more than adequately covered by Chow and Stintz. Thomson, as she had done four years previously, dropped out of the race. In 2014, she registered to run in for councillor in Ward 20. There was a crowded field in the downtown ward because there was no incumbent; Adam Vaughan had given up his council seat to run for the federal Liberals and was elected to the House of Commons in a by-election.

There was one major and totally unforeseen change that happened just moments before the cut-off for nominations at 2 p.m. on September 12. Ford withdrew from the race and his brother Doug, who had consistently said he was finished with politics after running his brother's campaign, entered.

On the morning of September 10, 2014, Rob and Doug were having breakfast together when Rob complained of severe abdominal pain. He went to his doctor and was immediately taken to Humber River Regional Hospital. Tests were done and it was determined he had a large tumor in his abdomen. The following day the mayor was transferred to Mount Sinai Hospital in downtown Toronto.

In the days that followed, it was announced the mayor's tumor was malignant. According to his lead physician, Dr. Zane Cohen, a colorectal specialist, Ford was suffering from a rare type of cancer, liposarcoma. The cancer was found not in any specific organ but in the fat cells. This made the cancer difficult to treat and more difficult to remove than had it been confined to a specific organ.

Cohen held a press conference to advise the public about the mayor's condition and although he would not indicate what the prognosis was, Ford later said his chances of beating the disease were 50/50.

Just prior to the close of nominations, Rob withdrew from the race but registered to run as a candidate for councillor in Ward 2, the position he had held in the 10 years prior to becoming mayor. Doug, who was planning to go back to the family business, Deco Labels and Tags, full time after the election registered to run for mayor.

When Doug initially decided not to run for council again, Michael Ford, the brothers' young nephew and Kathy Ford's son, entered the race in Ward 2. When Rob decided to run for his old council seat, Michael withdrew from the race and registered to run as a school trustee in Etobicoke.

Although there were five main candidates as the race got underway, Stintz and Soknacki never did break through. The race boiled down to three main candidates; Tory, Chow and one of the Ford brothers. When Doug entered the race, he began in second place in most of the polls, the same position Rob was in when he withdrew.

Olivia Chow

Chow was born in Hong Kong in 1957 and came to Canada with her parents and brother when she was 13 years of age. According to her biography, her parents had been educators in Hong Kong but could only find menial jobs once they immigrated. Her father worked at jobs such as driving a cab while her mother was a seamstress. Chow also indicates her father was abusive to her mother and brother but not to her. The father later suffered a nervous breakdown.

Chow was and still is a loyal member of the New Democratic Party. Unlike Mayor Miller, when Chow entered the race she did not quit the party and pretend she was now a centrist with no party affiliation just to get votes.

Chow began her political career by working for NDP MP Dan Heap in the leftist downtown area she had always represented during her lengthy political career. With Heap's support, she managed to get elected as a school board trustee in 1988. She served as a school trustee until 1991 when she was elected to Toronto City Council.

In 1988, Chow married Jack Layton who was a member of Toronto City Council. Layton would later run successfully for the federal NDP and was later chosen to lead the party. In the 2011 election, Layton was able to do what no other federal NDP leader had ever done; he led his party to a second place finish and became the first NDP leader to become Canada's leader of the Official Opposition. This was achieved by obtaining a large number of seats in the province of Quebec after Quebeckers became dissatisfied with all the other political parties, most notably the separatist Bloc Quebecois that virtually disappeared a few years after they had formed the Official Opposition.

Prior to the 2011 election, Layton announced he had prostate cancer and looked physically ill. Even though he was forced to use a cane, he undertook a gruelling 60-day campaign across the country that propelled his party into second place. In August 2011, a little over three months after the election, Layton passed away.

While a member of city council, Chow twice ran federally in Trinity-Spadina and was defeated by popular Liberal MP Tony Ianno. During her third try in 2006 when the country dumped the Liberals in favour of Stephen Harper's Conservative Party, Chow defeated Ianno by obtaining 28,748 votes to the incumbent's 25,067. Having resigned her council seat in November 2005, she went to join her husband in Ottawa. She remained a federal MP until giving up her seat to enter the mayor's race in March 2014.

Chow faced a couple of scandals during her council years. In 1990, Layton and Chow were living in a co-op in Toronto where rents are geared to income. With Layton as a councillor and Chow an elected school board trustee, the couple had a combined income of about $120,000 a year. Critics accused them of living in subsidized housing and feeding at the trough not only through their employment but in their housing as well. Although they were officially cleared of any wrongdoing, their subsequent actions spoke differently. Although they were paying $800 a month for rent they voluntarily increased their monthly payments adding over $300 a month to the amount of rent paid. While considered a great gesture by their friends and supporters, critics took this as proof positive that the rent they previously paid was below market and the cost of their unit was therefore being subsidized by the hardworking taxpayers of Toronto. If that wasn't enough, shortly after the scandal broke, the couple moved out. People wondered if they were not doing anything wrong and just complying with the co-op's mandate of having mixed income families residing there, why did they move out. This scandal, unknown by many of today's voters, became an issue during the 2014 mayoral campaign.

In 2000, Chow was a member of Toronto's Police Services Board while Mike Harris was premier of Ontario. The Harris years saw a lot of protests, demonstrations, and the odd riot protesting cuts the provincial government was making as well as the downloading of some costs of government from the province to municipalities.

On the day in question, the Ontario Coalition against Poverty (OCAP) were holding a large demonstration at Queen's Park. The demonstration turned into a riot with injuries and some people throwing marbles and other objects at the horses members of the Mounted Unit of the Toronto police were riding.

During the violence Chow road into Queen's Park on her trusty bicycle, later claiming she was only trying to help. According to police, she was instructing them what to do; to leave the protesters/rioters alone. Members of the Police Services board have no authority and in fact are prohibited by law from being involved in day to day policing activities. A report was prepared and Chow ended up resigning from the board.

During her political career, Chow championed issues of the left; women's rights, gay rights, homelessness and children's issues, giving little thought to where the money to pay for all these things would come from. She was a tax and spend leftist but like the Ford brothers and unlike Tory, there was no mistaking what she would do should she be elected mayor of Canada's largest city. It would be David Miller all over again.

After months of rumours and speculation that Chow would enter the race, she finally resigned her federal seat in Trinity-Spadina and formally entered the race in March 2014.

John Tory

John Tory was born in Toronto in 1954, the eldest son of John A. Tory, a prominent Toronto lawyer. The young Tory graduated law school and was called to the bar in 1980. He worked for his father's firm, (now Torys LLP) and not surprisingly made partner in the firm. He served as managing partner and was a member of the law firm's executive committee.

His business experience included his role in the telecommunications company, Rogers. Prior to his call to the bar, Tory worked for Rogers as a journalist between 1972 and 1979. He later went back to Rogers and served as the CEO of Rogers media from 1995 to 1999.

During his years running Rogers media, the negative billing controversy arose. In the early 1990s Rogers introduced the concept of negative billing whereby cable customers were automatically given additional channels at an increased cost. If customers did not want these other stations, the onus was on them to notify Rogers and cancel. People were outraged when the practice received wide publicity and the federal government later made negative billing illegal. Although negative billing had begun prior to Tory's assuming the position of CEO, he bore the brunt of the scandal as it was taking place. When he wasn't being called Mr. Rogers, he was often referred to as the "Cable Guy."

During the late 1990s, Tory served as commissioner of the Canadian Football League. While he and others credit him with saving the cash-strapped league, he is best known for expanding the Canadian league into the United States. None of the American teams lasted too long and Tory was blamed for what appeared to many football fans, a ridiculous idea. The Canadian game is different than its American counterpart with a 55 yard field and three downs instead of four. Tory expanded the league in a country where college and even high school football are extremely popular. It seemed doomed at the outset. Tory earned $1 a year as commissioner and some joked he was overpaid.

Politically, Tory was a member of both the federal and Ontario Progressive Conservative Party. In the early 1980s, Tory served as principle secretary to then Ontario Premier Bill Davis. He also worked for PC Prime Minister Brian Mulroney.

When Mulroney stepped down and was replaced by Kim Campbell, Tory became Campbell's campaign manager when she sought to be elected prime minister of Canada in her own right. It was during this campaign that Tory approved an ad many consider was the nastiest negative campaign ad in Canadian history.

The ad showed a close up of Liberal leader Jean Chrétien while asking if this man looks like a prime minister. Chrétien has a facial deformity that makes one side of his mouth droop. Although jokes had been made about the fact the Quebec MP looks like the driver of a getaway car, at that point Chrétien had never spoken publicly about his facial deformity. After the ad aired, Chrétien, who would go on to easily win the 1993 election, said he had suffered from Bell's palsy as a boy that caused one side of his mouth to droop.

In a weak attempt to defend the ad, Tory showed the media published close ups of Chrétien's face to show the Campbell ad was no different. Of course these other pictures of the 30-year veteran of Parliament were not accompanied by any captions about his looks.

Candidate Campbell stated she had not authorized the negative ad and it was pulled shortly after it was aired.

This and subsequent political decisions Tory has made provided clear evidence that his political instincts leave a lot to be desired. And when it comes to political smarts Chrétien, love him or hate him, is Tory's polar opposite.

After the ad aired, Chrétien addressed the media. Shrugging his shoulders, the Liberal leader said his face was the one God had given him.

Then he quipped that although he speaks out of the side of his mouth, at least he doesn't speak out of both sides of his mouth like the Progressive Conservatives do. Even to Chrétien's political enemies, he showed grace, class and, without appearing to be angry, put down the ad Tory thought was a good way to win votes.

After the votes were counted, the once mighty PC Party that had been around since Confederation in 1867, was reduced to just two seats. After eight years of majority rule under the Mulroney government, Canadians were really fed up and wanted a change. Campbell was destined to lose from the outset and although it is difficult to say what would have happened if, the PCs may have done at least a little better had the attack ad not brought sympathy and respect for the Liberal leader.

The disastrous showing marked the beginning of the end of the PCs. What was left of it later merged with the Canadian Alliance Party (previously the Reform Party) to form the Conservative Party of Canada that is currently in power today. How much of this can be attributed to Tory is unknown, but his vicious ad certainly did not help.

In 1995, the Ontario Progressive Conservative Party under Mike Harris, to the surprise of many, seemed to come out of nowhere to win a majority government. Harris, an unabashed small "c" conservative shocked many when he began to implement the fiscally conservative policies he campaigned on. Known as the "Common Sense Revolution," Harris set out to cut social assistance rates, introduced a workfare program and cut taxes. The Common Sense Revolution led to frequent demonstrations, labour disruptions, and the odd riot such as the one that cost Chow her position on the Toronto Police Services Board. Those dependent upon the largesse of government for their survival and the many special interest groups including civil servants were not a happy lot.

After winning a second majority in 1999, Harris stepped down for personal reasons in 2002 and was replaced by Ernie Eves who had served as his Minister of Finance. In the provincial election held the following year, Eves and the PCs were trounced by the Liberal Party of Ontario under Dalton

McGuinty. Later that year, Eves stepped down and the party was led by interim leader Bob Runciman.

In 2003, after Mel Lastman, the first mayor of the amalgamated city of Toronto announced he would not seek re-election, Tory ran for mayor of Toronto. He finished in second place behind Miller but beat out former Toronto mayor Barbara Hall and former Liberal MP John Nunziata.

In September 2004, Tory ran for and won the leadership of the PC Party of Ontario. At that time he had never held elective office. In both the mayoral run and the successful bid to become the PC leader, Tory proved himself to be one of these people who had absolutely no interest in running for lowly elected office such as school board trustee, city councillor, or MPP. It was the top job or nothing.

After Eves resigned his seat, Tory ran in the by-election to fill the vacant seat. In 2005, after winning the leadership, Tory was elected as MPP of Dufferin-Peel-Wellington-Grey, outside of Toronto. It was a safe Conservative seat and despite being parachuted into a riding he had no connection to, he managed to win getting around 56% of the vote.

But during his years as leader of a provincial political party, Tory cemented his reputation as a loser. Of the 2007 provincial election campaign and election, many conservatives referred to Tory as snatching defeat from the jaws of victory.

Although only in power for four years, Premier Dalton McGuinty was not a shoo-in to be re-elected. During the previous election campaign in 2003, McGuinty looked straight into the camera and promised Ontarians they would not pay one penny more in taxes than they were paying under the Progressive Conservative government. After being rewarded with a majority government, McGuinty imposed the largest tax increase in the province's history by introducing a new health tax. Years before the scandals such as eHealth, Ornge and when the Liberals later admitted they relocated two gas plants under construction to save two seats in the 2011 campaign, McGuinty was vulnerable because of his lies. The premier was often portrayed as Pinocchio. Tory was a "Red Tory," someone who was slightly more fiscally conservative than the Liberals but who would never be confused with a real conservative like Harris. The province was ripe for the return of the PCs albeit in perhaps in a kinder and gentler form than the Harris government was.

Both historically and under Canada's constitution, Roman Catholics are sometimes subject to different treatment than other Canadians. Under the *Constitution Act, 1867,* drafted as a condition of confederation, there is a section that says nothing in the constitution can adversely affect the rights and privileges enjoyed by Roman Catholics prior to confederation. It was a condition required by Lower Canada (Quebec) in order to form the country. As a result of this anomaly, Ontario has two school boards, public and separate (Catholic) schools that are both funded by the government.

Tory decided to make government funding available for all religious schools the main plank in his 2007 election campaign. Although discussions about Roman Catholic school funding is spoken about from time to time, it was not an issue in the minds of most Ontarians in 2007. With the exception of the PC leader, few if any voters in Ontario were going to bed and unable to sleep because Catholic schools were publicly funded while Jewish schools and Muslim schools and Hindu schools were not. The Liberals won another majority, winning 71 seats. McGuinty, gaining quite the reputation as a liar, saw his government only down one seat. Were it not for a major issue ordinary Ontarians cared nothing about, the results might have been vastly different.

To make matters worse, in the general election Tory decided he did not want to run in Eves' old safe riding where the rubes live, preferring to run in the high class Leaside area of Toronto where his kind of people live. His Liberal opponent was Kathleen Wynne who served the area as a school trustee and MPP. Wynne was a popular cabinet minister in McGuinty's government and would go on to succeed him as premier and later win a majority government in her own right. While the Liberals may have been vulnerable due to McGuinty's breaking of promises, especially his one on tax increases, the Liberals were not yet at the stage where voters wanted to throw all the bums out. Tory's arrogance and lack of political smarts showed after he gave up a safe seat where he was the incumbent in an attempt to beat a popular Liberal MPP.

When the ballots were counted, Wynne won her riding of Don Valley West garnering 23,059 votes to Tory's second place finish where he obtained 18,136 votes. The leader of the official opposition was seatless again. He would lead his party from the sidelines for another 17 months.

At the beginning of 2009, PC MPP Laurie Scott announced she was stepping down from her seat in the riding of Haliburton-Kawartha Lakes-Brock, just northeast of Toronto. The former nurse first won the riding in 2003 and easily won again in 2007. This seat, like the one previously held by Eves, was considered a safe Progressive Conservative seat and was last held by the Liberals in 1994.

Scott vacated her seat in exchange for a severance payment of $100,000. Her stepping down paved the way for Tory to run after the premier called a by-election.

The by-election was called for March 5, 2009. To the shock of some, Tory again lost his bid to obtain a seat in the Ontario legislature. He finished two percentage points or about 1,000 votes behind Liberal Rick Johnson. This loss, coupled with his loss to Wynne two years before, cemented his reputation as a loser. The day after the by-election, Tory announced he was stepping down as PC leader.

Tory then went to work for *Newstalk1010*, a major Toronto radio station where he hosted the afternoon drive home talk show. Tory remained there until he formally entered the 2014 campaign for mayor, spending much of his final months criticizing Rob Ford. He had the tremendous advantage of using his show to campaign for mayor on the airwaves. Since he had not formally declared his candidacy, there was nothing illegal about what he did.

Tory was rumoured to have seriously thought about entering the 2010 race for Toronto mayor although he declined doing so since Ford decided to run. During that campaign, he had some wonderful things to say about Rob and Doug Ford.

Tory also remained active in civic causes including becoming the chair of the Greater Toronto Civic Action Committee. With his work outside elected politics, it became clear to close observers that he was just as comfortable if not more, working with Liberals who he opposed as leader of the PCs rather than with conservatives. He appeared to have an especially close relationship with Wynne who easily beat him in 2007 and who would succeed McGuinty and lead her party to a majority government in 2014. In February 2014, Tory officially entered the Toronto mayor's race. He appeared to be whatever people wanted him to be; to those on the left, he was a conservative and for those on the right, he was a leftie. Some conservatives, Ford supporters, began to refer to him as John "Liberal" rather than John Tory.

Doug Ford

The older brother of Rob, Doug had more than 25 years of business experience before first running for elective office in 2010. Doug took a much more active role in the family business, Deco Tags and Labelling, than Rob did. Doug worked his way up in the company and eventually became president. He was responsible for expanding the business by opening a branch in Chicago and buying another company in New Jersey. Doug took over full control of Deco after his father's death in 2006.

Like other members of his family, Doug was involved in community service and charitable work. He was a member of the Toronto West Rotary Club for more than 20 years.

He was a large supporter of Rob while the latter was a city councillor and when Rob announced he would run for mayor in the 2010 campaign, Doug decided to run for council in Ward 2, the ward held by his brother for the previous 10 years. Out of 17,662 valid votes cast in the Etobicoke ward, Doug received 12,660, approximately 10,000 more votes than his nearest rival obtained. After the election the rookie councillor announced he would donate his entire salary to community organizations.

When the mayor announced he would seek re-election in 2014, Doug announced he would manage his brother's campaign but would not run for re-election to city council. He would end his political career and return to the family business and be able to spend more time with his wife and daughters.

When the mayor became seriously ill two days before the deadline to run or formally withdraw from the municipal race, the Ford brothers did a switch. Doug registered to run for mayor while Rob withdrew and entered the race for councillor in his old ward.

The only major scandal to hit the older brother was when the *Globe and Mail* revealed he had sold hash during the 1980s. The story, published in May, 2013, was based on several anonymous sources and Ford denied he had trafficked in the substance. While these allegations pertained to Doug, it was not the only time the elite media published material detrimental to the Fords based upon anonymous sources. They clearly did not like the Fords.

While the two brothers shared the same political philosophy of stopping the gravy train, respect for taxpayers and subways, subways, subways, they are two different people. Doug is a teetotaller and there was no evidence he used drugs apart from what the media reported took place 30 years ago. While Rob weighed around 300 pounds and his visits to KFC would be videotaped and reported by the media, Doug is a vegetarian. He said he has been a vegetarian since his youth when he worked in a meat packing facility.

Doug was his brother's biggest defender. While his enemies often accused him of lying in order to defend Rob, the reality is the brothers were not as close as many believed. When news of the existence of the crack video first surfaced, Doug strongly defended his brother, saying he did not smoke crack and the allegations that he did was a plot by the *Toronto Star* to discredit him. Of course, later, Rob admitted to having smoked crack in one of his drunken stupors. Doug has the ability to be more combative in defense of his brother than Rob does.

When the police investigation into the mayor's activities became known, Doug accused Chief Blair of going after Rob for political reasons. At one point, Blair threatened the councillor with a libel action and Doug apologized.

Doug, the father of four daughters who did not even drink alcohol, was never known to frequent the areas or hang around the same people as his brother did, preferring to spend time with his family. He likely had no knowledge of many of his brother's activities and merely accepted Rob's earlier denials that he never used crack.

While Doug is popular with members of Ford Nation for his political views, he does not have the same charisma as his brother. Like other councillors, he did not take off in a flash to visit people who had made complaints about problems they were having. Unlike his brother, Doug did not make his cellphone available so his constituents could easily reach him. While popular, he did not receive the same superstar status as Rob where people would line up to have their pictures taken with him. Although we will never know for certain, it has been speculated that even with all the scandals, Rob would have obtained more votes had he been physically able to continue in the mayor's race. Rob was seen more much more likeable than his older brother who was frequently abrupt and labelled by the mainstream media as a bully.

Prior to announcing his intention to leave politics, Doug expressed a desire to run for the provincial PCs in the election held on June 12, 2014. His hopes were dashed when then PC leader Tim Hudak refused to allow him to run.

During that election, Hudak took a page out of John Tory's book and snatched defeat from the jaws of victory. During the early days of the campaign and without telling party members and candidates about it, Hudak announced he was going to cut the Ontario public service by 100,000 jobs. Instead of speaking about buyouts or attrition, he came across as wanting to fire 100,000 public servants. And he seemed to be enjoying the prospect. One feature of the province's public service is that it is indeed bloated. Civil servants are everywhere. As a result, many people sympathetic to the need for smaller governments have spouses, relatives, friends and neighbours who work for the Ontario government and don't want to see these people fired just for the sake of firing them. The Liberal government, seen by all but the truest Liberal supporters as corrupt, ended up going from minority to majority status as a result of the poor campaign run by both the PCs and the NDP. After the election Hudak announced he would not lead the party in the next provincial election. The backlash was so great he was forced to resign as party leader and an interim leader was chosen.

After the October 27 municipal election, Doug announced he was seriously considering running for the PC leadership to replace Hudak. He would have been a formidable leadership candidate and a true conservative among Republican establishment-like candidates. While the Progressive Conservatives had around 100,000 members at one point, that number had dropped to about 10,000. The next leader of the party will be the person who can sell the most memberships. Doug could count on not only the members of Ford Nation but true fiscal conservatives outside of Toronto who wished they had politicians like the Ford brothers.

One day in late November, Doug announced he would be holding a press conference later in the day to announce his decision. Usually in situations like this, holding a press conference would be a signal he was going to enter the race. If he had decided not to run he could have just issued a media release.

While telling this to his viewers on *CP24*, Stephen LeDrew chuckled and said since this was one of the Fords making the announcement, he could end up announcing he was not going to run. And LeDrew was right.

Doug said he would not be entering the leadership race. He wanted to spend more time with his family and the leadership run and being party leader if elected would entail a lot of travel throughout the province. But he did not rule out running as a PC candidate in the Etobicoke riding once held by his later father when the next election is called.

By March, 2014, the five major candidates in the mayor's race were in place. The way the media portrayed the mayoral wannabes, Chow was on the left or centre left while Ford, Tory, Soknacki and Stintz were all on the right or centre right. It was no contest and the Ford-hating left wing media pretty well declared Chow the winner and the 65th mayor of the city of Toronto. With the right split, there was no way she could lose. It was only a matter of time before the type of city government Miller ran and the left love, would return.

There was something to the media's division of the five main mayoral candidates. Ford was just as obsessed with fiscal conservatism and the spending of other peoples' money by the city as he was when he was first elected to council in 2000. And Tory's last political gig, although a total flop, was as leader of Ontario's Progressive Conservative Party, at least perceived to be more fiscally conservative than the governing Liberals and the third party NDP. Soknacki, a businessman who was prudent enough to move his own business from Toronto to Markham to avoid the high business taxes in the city, was also seen as being fiscally conservative despite the fact he had served as budget chief during one of Miller's terms. And Stintz too, was seen as a fiscal conservative and as mayor, would not have spent taxpayers' money in the same way the NDP's Chow would. But she was no Ford. During her first term on council she spent thousands of taxpayer dollars so she could learn French. Despite French being an official language of Canada, very few Torontonians speak French compared to other languages such as Mandarin, Spanish and Urdu. But she was no flaming socialist when it came to spending and could be properly placed on the right of centre.

The campaigns of both Soknacki and Stintz failed to take off and both dropped out of the race before the deadline to officially withdraw came. While in the race, Stintz and Soknacki continued to poll in the low single digits. The real race was a three way one between one of the Ford brothers, Tory and Chow.

As the race began it appeared the media was correct; Chow jumped into the lead while the scandal-plagued incumbent placed second. Tory was well behind in third place.

As for Ford, although it was a new year and a new campaign, the scandals that dogged him during most of the previous year continued. It seemed reports of the existence of the crack video, his acknowledgement of smoking crack during one of his drunken stupors and the revelation that he was under a police investigation aggravated his substance abuse problems.

Only three weeks into the New Year and the formal campaign, a new video surfaced. This one showed Ford, obviously inebriated, at Steak Queen, a fast food restaurant in the Rexdale area of Etobicoke. On the tape, the mayor can be seen speaking Jamaican Patois and while his critics quickly labelled that as another act of racism, the Jamaicans who were in the restaurant at the time, did not seem to mind. What was more troubling was that he was swearing, often using the Patois word "bumbaclot" which is slang for toilet paper and used in place of the word "f**k." If that wasn't enough, Ford is heard on the video calling Toronto Police Chief Bill Blair a "c**ks****r," and talking incoherently about counter-surveillance.

Another video from Steak Queen that night, showed an apparently normal-looking Ford sitting in a booth talking to his friend Lisi. The *National Post* later wrote that this video was the more disturbing of the two shot that night. It showed him not only still associating with unsavoury people but at that time, Lisi was facing the outstanding extortion charge having to do with the crack video.

Ford later admitted to being drunk that evening but refused to answer the media's questions about whether he had taken drugs or if he had driven himself to and from Steak Queen.

The end of the month saw Scott MacIntyre launch a civil law suit against Ford. In 2012, MacIntyre, who was married to the mayor's sister, Kathy, was in jail at the Toronto West Detention Centre when he was beaten by other inmates. MacIntyre was jailed after he went to Ford's home, had a confrontation with the mayor, and threatened to kill him.

In his suit, MacIntyre claimed the beating was instigated by the mayor in order to keep him quiet about Ford's alcohol and drug use. None of these allegations have yet been proven. Ford's lawyer, Dennis Morris, described the mayor's involvement in the beating as "insanity."

At the end of April, still another video surfaced. Although the person who had it failed in an attempt to sell it to the media, clips of the video were released. The tape was purported to have been recent and showed Ford appearing to smoke something from a metal pipe that could have been either crack cocaine or marijuana. It was also claimed the video was shot in the basement of Ford's sister Kathy's home. MacIntyre confirmed the location and said the pipe was the same type Kathy used to smoke crack. Reporters with the *Globe and Mail* said they had seen the entire video.

Around the same as this video surfaced, an audio tape was released by the media. On the tape, Ford is heard making anti-gay remarks and saying of fellow councillor and candidate Karen Stintz that he would like to "jam her."

After these tapes surfaced, Ford announced he would go into rehab. Under city council rules, a member who misses three consecutive meetings can be removed from office unless permission is granted for the absences. The same councillors who had been calling for Ford to resign and who voted to strip the mayor of all the powers they could, unanimously voted to allow Ford to miss sittings of council and still retain his position as mayor.

Ford took off for Chicago presumably to seek treatment but immediately returned. It is believed he was denied entry into the United States because of his admitted drug use. The mayor ended up going to GreenStone Clinic, a rehabilitation facility in Ontario's cottage country north of Toronto. Ford spent two months at GreenStone, returning to Toronto and the campaign at the beginning of July.

Despite the fact the family requested privacy while the mayor sought help for his substance abuse problems, the media wasted no time descending on GreenStone hoping to get some news to further discredit Ford. There was talk of some media outlets attempting or at least considering getting someone admitted to the facility in order to get information about the mayor.

The only incident of note while at GreenStone happened when Ford lent his vehicle to a fellow patient who proceeded to be pulled over in Ford's car by the police and charged with impaired driving. As is mandatory under Ontario law, Ford's Cadillac Escalade was seized and taken to an impound lot. Such was the obsession of the media with Ford that pictures of his lonely Escalade sitting in an impound lot became big news.

The media criticized the mayor any time he left the clinic to go into the town of Gravenhurst or even walk outside the hospital grounds. As many people correctly noted, he was not in jail but voluntarily receiving treatment and he, like the other patients, was allowed to leave the clinic's grounds with permission without running the risk of being kicked out of the facility. Like in Toronto, when he went out in public during rehab, he was mobbed by fans and posed for pictures with them.

After Ford left GreenStone and returned to the campaign trail, many including his supporters were waiting for him to relapse as is common with recovering addicts. But to the disappointment of his enemies, he was never again seen in public either drunk or high on drugs. It was impossible any drug use or excessive drinking could have escaped the constant prying eyes of the media when the mayor resumed campaigning.

Gradually the platforms of the three major candidates emerged. Those of Rob and later Doug were no surprise. They campaigned on the same ideas and with the same slogans that Rob successfully rode to victory on in 2010; stopping the gravy train, respect for taxpayers and subways, subways, subways.

Chow's platform was no surprise either. A hard core NDP leftist she said it all at the outset of the campaign. When asked by the *Toronto Star's* Daniel Dale how she differed from Mayor David Miller she said she was not a male and not white. Not only would she govern as Miller had but she would play the race and gender card. During the first half of the campaign it worked. Doing what's best "for the children" with no regard to where the money would come from was a centerpiece of her platform.

Tory made transit, his SmartTrack plan, the centerpiece of his campaign. He also stressed that he would bring Torontonians together and end the circus. In other words, he was not and would not become Rob Ford. Tory also claimed he was the only one of the candidates who could successfully work with other levels of government and end the circus that had encompassed the final months of Rob Ford's tenure as mayor. Critics accused the former PC of being too close to the premier and her Liberal Party.

The following were the candidates' positions on major issues facing the voters.

Transit and Gridlock

For the fourth largest city in North America that likes to refer to itself as a world class city, Toronto is severely lacking in subways. There is essentially one major north-south line and one east-west one. Another north-south line runs almost parallel with the main line but in the downtown core the two lines service pretty well the same area.

The most recent line, opened under the Lastman administration, runs east-west along Sheppard Avenue in the northern part of the city. It runs for a few stops and then comes to an abrupt end. It does not service commuters west of the dividing line of Yonge Street and does not travel into Scarborough to service the residents of that area. This track is often called "the subway to nowhere."

Pretty well everyone is agreed, the city needs more public transit. The battles before council and during the last election campaign were over subways vs. light rail transit (LRT).

Proponents of LRT argue it is much cheaper than tunnelling underground and therefore more public transit can be built for the same money. Those who favour subways argue they are more conducive to Canadian winters, will not disrupt motor vehicle traffic and negatively impact on local businesses and will give people living in the northeast part of the city (Scarborough) closer access to the subway lines that are so handy to those living in the downtown core. As well, there was a lot of controversy over the new streetcar line built along St. Clair Avenue during the Miller administration. That project has been criticized for reducing parking spaces, vehicle lanes, and being disruptive of the small mom and pop businesses that operate on the street.

There is also talk about constructing a downtown relief line that would run somewhat parallel to the main north-south lines to reduce the crowding, especially at rush hour.

Currently, construction is underway on Eglinton Avenue that runs east west. Although it is a LRT line, much of it will be built underground. Plans are also in the works for LRT lines along Finch Avenue and Sheppard Avenue that run east-west in the northern part of Toronto.

Chow was the only one of the major candidates to oppose the construction of the Scarborough subway and favoured building an LRT rather than a subway. She also supported all other LTR projects planned for Toronto.

Chow promised if elected she would put more buses on the streets during rush hour to ease overcrowding. The tax and spend socialist would increase the Land Transfer Tax to fund this project. One of the criticisms of this plan was that the additional buses would add to the congestion on the already gridlocked streets.

Like Chow, Tory favoured light rail lines on Sheppard, Finch and Eglinton but was in favour of the construction of the Scarborough subway. When pressed, he said was in favour of a downtown relief line but did not seem to make it a priority. The need for this relief line has been talked about for years.

A major plank of Tory's mayoral campaign was his SmartTrack plan. Under this proposal, a 22-stop light rail line would be constructed using existing provincial GO Train tracks that would have to be electrified. This would require the consent of the province, but another major platform in his campaign was that he was best suited to work with others, including the provincial and federal governments who would be asked to contribute to Toronto's transit system. Tory's figures on the cost of SmartTrack were questioned during the campaign and much of the details of the monies required were unknown to the former PC leader. It was also pointed out to Tory, that the lines on his SmartTrack line would have to travel through an apartment building. Some suspected Tory, who was now extremely close to the current Liberal Party premier, had already received her okay for the proposal. The SmartTrack line would also extend outside the city's boundaries causing some to question if his plan would help the province more than the city.

Doug Ford would continue his and his brother's mantra of "subways, subways, subways." He was not only in favour of the Scarborough subway but wanted subways on Sheppard and Finch and would bury that part of the Eglinton LRT that is being constructed above ground.

Like the other candidates, he was questioned about his estimated cost of all these subways. At least in the long term, there was appeal for more subways rather than light rail lines.

When it came to the related issue of gridlock, Chow called for traffic lights to be better synchronized, and greater enforcement of laws against idling and blocking intersections. Chow also proposed construction companies that block roads while no work is being done should be subjected to fines although these fines, if they became a reality, would obviously be passed down to the ultimate consumer.

Like Chow, Tory advocated better traffic light systems to reduce the impeding of vehicle traffic. He also called for better coordination of construction on city streets in order to minimize delays. Tory also wanted Toronto to crack down on illegal parking and stopping although how this would affect the many commercial vehicles who make daily deliveries in the downtown core is not known.

At one time, Tory toyed with the idea of using Lake Ontario for the purpose of transporting residents by boat from one end of the city to the other.

Ford was also in favour of better technology in the coordination of traffic signals.

Taxes

When it came to property taxes, all candidates used the rate of inflation as an initial measurement of these taxes. Chow promised to hold property tax increases to "around" the rate of inflation without exactly defining what she meant by "around." In a "tax the rich" promise socialist and liberal tax and spenders are so fond of, she proposed increasing the Land Transfer Tax by an additional 1% on homes with a selling price of over $2 million. Chow also proposed decreasing business taxes on small businesses.

Tory promised to hold any increase in property taxes to the rate of inflation or below and was in favour of leaving the Land Transfer Tax as it is.

Doug Ford promised if elected, he would keep any property tax increases below the rate of inflation and would slash the LTT by 15% a year for four years.

Contracting Out of Garbage Collection

One of Ford's initial acts as mayor was to contract out the collection of garbage west of Yonge Street that is considered to be the east-west dividing line of the city. Chow was not in favour of contracting out the collection of garbage on the grounds that competition was needed. She never did explain why this competition that would be in the best interests of Torontonians could not be provided by another private company rather than highly paid unionized city workers.

Although the city's unions dispute this, the contacting out of collection has saved the city just under $12 million a year since its inception. Unlike Chow, both Tory and Ford were in favour of further contracting out.

Pride Parade

Toronto is home to one of the world's largest gay pride festivals and the parade and surrounding events brings millions of dollars into the city. Although it should not have become an important campaign issue, it did so due to Rob Ford's alleged homophobia. There was an attempt to paint Doug as being just like his brother although there was no record of him making homophobic remarks.

The parade is held on a weekend at the end of June and as mayor, Rob never attended let alone marched in the parade as most politicians do. Rather than say that the parade contains a lot of nudity and he feels uncomfortable, he would use the excuse that this was the weekend he always spends at the cottage with his family. One year he refused to attend the parade even after someone agreed to charter a plane to fly him from the cottage and then take him back. Doug had been to the parade but Fords' enemies tried their best to paint him as anti-gay.

Much of what is known as the Rob Ford scandal involves the making sexist and homophobic remarks as well as racist remarks directed at blacks, Jews, and Asians. On one of the tapes, the mayor is overheard calling federal Liberal leader Justin Trudeau, "a fag." He was also heard using the term "fucking minorities" although in context he was using the F-word for emphasis.

In many of the debates between the major players (there were over 65 of them) and in the media this issue of the parade was often raised. Doug said he has gone to the parade in the past although he stopped short of saying he would march in it if elected mayor.

The last few years, a group called Queers Against Israeli Apartheid (QuAIA) was allowed to participate in the parade. Last year, city bureaucrats ruled the group's presence did not breach any of the city's policies. As the parade and festivities are funded in large part by the city, the question of the group's presence has been an issue.

Other than gay rights, bashing Israel is the only political event during Pride Week. There is never any mention of countries that jail, torture and kill people because of their sexual orientation. Only Israel, the only Middle East democracy that holds similar parades, is singled out for criticism. Given the nature of this, the presence of QuAIA at the parade can easily be seen as supporting anti-Semitism.

Chow being a committed leftist and member of the NDP has no problem with QuAIA taking part in the gay pride parade. Both Tory and Ford said if elected, they would cut funding to the events if the QuAIA are allowed to march in the parade.

Children and Daycare

Chow made "the children" a major part of her election platform. She promised if elected, she would see to it that an additional 36,000 Toronto children would be fed at school at a cost of about $2 million a year. Why these 36,000 children needed to be fed by the state instead of their parents was never explained.

Tory, taking his middle of the road approach in order to please everybody, promised he would work with other levels of government to try and increase school breakfast programs. And Ford had really no comment on feeding children at school.

On daycare, true to her tax and spend roots, Chow said she would spend $15 million a year and create 3,000 new daycare spaces. She also promised to create more after school programs. Where all this money would come from did not seem to be a concern for her.

Tory said he wasn't sure the city had the money for more daycare but would try and get money from other levels of government. Ford also said he would try and get additional money from the province to use on childcare.

There were of course many more policies on everything from the environment to jobs to economic development, but these few give a general idea of differences between the major candidates, especially on the important issue of transit.

How the candidates fared during the election campaign

After Chow entered the race in March she was off to a firm first place standing making the media proud of their prediction. Rob was a respectable second with Tory trailing in third.

Although the candidates' actual support went up and down in the various polls, these positions remained the same until late May when the revelations that forced Rob into rehab surfaced. Polls then showed, him neck and neck with Tory with the third place candidate sometimes overtaking him. Chow led until the summer when she and Tory traded places. To the horror of some, the obvious winner at the outset of a race was far back in third place. The woman who at the outset of the campaign was predicted to be Toronto's next mayor was trailing the bigoted, drunken crackhead.

Two reasons were given for Chow's fall from grace. One was that Rob left the campaign and went into rehab for two months. While he remained the centre of attention in the media that constantly speculated about what and how well he was doing and waiting for another scandal to emerge, he was not involved in the debates or the day-to-day campaign. This allowed more attention to be focused on the other two major candidates.

Chow was seen as being out of touch and having little knowledge of municipal issues despite her long history as serving as a school board trustee and councillor. She advocated the city bring in a gun ban, something floated during the Miller administration. While such a bylaw would be possible, it was not a proper municipal function; firearms and their regulation fall within the jurisdiction of the federal government. And as far as crime in the city is concerned, criminals who possess and use illegal firearms despite facing possible prison terms were not likely to give up their guns because of a city bylaw akin to parking at an expired meter.

After a pedestrian was killed at an intersection, Chow suggested having square curbs erected at intersections to keep vehicles away from the curb. She obviously gave no thought to how this would affect her beloved buses that she promised more of. Or emergency vehicles and the large trucks that deliver to the left's favourite cafes.

While Chow was born in Hong Kong, she has been in Canada since 1970. When more attention was placed on her, more and more people realized how poor her English language skills are and her inability to properly communicate. For example she would often mix up tenses referring to "women" as "woman."

With more attention paid to Tory, he came across as a more reasonable alternative for the ABF (Anybody but Ford) crowd. As a former Progressive Conservative leader, he was seen as being much more fiscally conservative than Chow. And being a "Red Tory," there was very little difference between him and a Liberal, the preferred Ontario party in Toronto. In fact the who's who of the Ontario Liberal Party, the ones he once opposed in the legislature, flocked to endorse him.

There was a second reason why Chow had dropped in the polls. Wynne, whose government is considered to be the most corrupt in the history of the province, called a snap election that was held on June 12. The blunders of PC leader Tim Hudak made it clear he was not likely to form the next government and Wynne and the Liberals would be re-elected. What was not anticipated by many was that when the ballots were counted, Wynne's party went from a minority to form a majority government. Liberal Party support was especially strong in the city of Toronto.

Despite Hudak's major blunder that had even his candidates shaking their heads, the success of forming a majority government also came from the relatively poor showing of the provincial NDP. Traditional party supporters were angered by what was seen as leader Andrea Horwath's move to the centre. Whether Horwath did in fact move to the center or Wynne, by campaigning on policies such as a provincial pension plan, outflanked the NDP on the left, the party did not do well.

Federally, with the rise of Liberal leader Justin Trudeau, the NDP that now forms the official opposition, are losing ground. Some speculate this and what happened in Ontario marks the beginning of the end of the New Democratic Party. That may be an exaggeration but the party's decline in popularity did not help Chow.

The absence of Ford during rehab enabled more attention to be paid to Chow. Despite her long political career, until her run for mayor she had never sought elective office outside of the small downtown area that now encompasses Trinity-Spadina that traditionally made the NDP a major player.

This stronghold seemed to slip away after a by-election was called to replace Chow who gave up her federal seat to run for mayor. Joe Cressy, the NDP candidate, lost to Adam Vaughan, a former councillor and journalist who ran for the Liberals. Vaughan obtained 53% of the vote compared to Cressy, a well-known NDP activist, who obtained only 34%. Cressy would later go on to be elected councillor for Ward 20, the same ward Vaughan represented until he resigned his seat to run federally.

Both of these factors; more attention paid to Chow and disenchantment within the NDP base, led to Chow's downfall to third place where she would remain and finish after the ballots were counted.

After Rob pulled out of the race to be replaced by Doug, Doug at first increased the second place lead Rob had held before his cancer diagnosis. But as October 27 neared, polls continued to show Tory pulling away from Ford.

As voting day approached, all four major Toronto newspapers; the *Toronto Sun*, the *Toronto Star*, the *National Post* and the *Globe and Mail*, endorsed Tory for mayor. This angered many Torontonians on the left who thought the *Star* should have endorsed Chow and those on the right who thought the *Sun*, known for its right wing populism, should have endorsed Ford. But the media were all in agreement; Ford had to go and Tory was the best choice to succeed him.

Election Day – October 27, 2014

After a record turnout at the advanced polls held at various locations throughout the city, approximately 60% of eligible voters turned up to vote. This included many people who usually do not pay attention to municipal politics and do not bother voting. While many of these people voted in order to prevent another Ford from becoming mayor, other traditional non-voters showed up to support not only Doug but Rob as well.

When the votes were counted, Tory became mayor-elect although his lead over second place Doug was not as much as the most recent polls had predicted. Tory took 40.3% of the votes compared to Doug's 33.7%. While some of the latter polls had Tory leading Ford by more than 14 points, in the end less than 7% separated them. Chow finished a distant third with 23.2%. The only consolation for Chow that evening is that she doubled the percentage of the vote obtained by Pantalone in 2010. The election of Chow or Pantalone in 2010, would have signalled the return to or continuation of Miller's policies of tax increases, caving into the city's unionized workers, and spending time and money on non-municipal issues such as climate change and gun control.

An election map of the city showed Chow won her previous ward of Trinity-Spadina as well as two neighbouring downtown wards, Davenport and Parkdale High Park. Tory won the rest of the centre of the city all the way up to the northern border of Toronto. The mayor-elect also won four wards in the south of Etobicoke as well as one in the south of Scarborough. These southern wards are all adjacent to the old city of Toronto. The remainder of the suburbs went to Ford.

Both Rob and Mike Ford easily won. After Rob decided to run for his and Doug's old council seat, he campaigned very little, only knocking on doors in between chemotherapy treatments if he felt up to it. Rob managed to obtain 11,629 votes from the 19,793 valid ballots cast. Andray Domise, endorsed by many in the media to succeed the crack-smoking drunken Ford, came a distant third getting only 1.620 votes.

And then there was Michael Ford, Kathy's son and nephew of Rob and Doug. After initially running for Doug's old council seat in Ward 2, he dropped out to let Rob run while he himself registered to run for school trustee of the Toronto District School Board in Etobicoke North that encompasses Wards 1 and 2. While he was on the ballot first as a council candidate and later to run for the school board, the 20-year-old Ford gave no media interviews and did not even have a website. He spent all his time knocking on doors. After the election he said his prime qualification to be a school board trustee is that it had not been that long since he had been in high school.

After the ballots were tallied, Michael won with about 44% of the vote. It was almost double the number of votes received by the second-place finisher, John Hastings, 72. Hasting was the incumbent trustee who held the position since 2006 and had previously served as a PC MPP under the Harris and Eves government between 1995 and 2003.

The next municipal election will be held in 2018. About the mayoral campaign in that election, Rob, referred to as "the Fordinator" by the

Toronto Sun, said, "I'll be back." While undergoing chemotherapy for cancer, Rob told the media he was plotting a return to run for mayor in four years. If his health permits, there is little doubt he will take another run at the city's top job.

Doug is out of politics but may return during the next provincial campaign in an attempt to win his father's old seat. Contrary to the wishes of the Ford-haters, although John Tory is now the mayor of Toronto the Fords are not going away.

Part II – Ford Nation

Chapter 6

The Fords Retain Significant Support

When the official results of the 2014 mayoral race were tabulated, Doug ended up with 331,006 votes. Tory, the successful candidate received 395,124 votes and Chow finished third with 227,003 votes. Toronto criminal lawyer Ari Goldkind, who took part in some of the media debates until Doug refused to participate if Goldkind was there, finished way behind in fourth place, getting only 3,916 votes.

No matter how you look at it Doug finished a respectable second capturing the votes of almost a third of a million Torontonians.

It is impossible to know what would have happened if... How would Rob have done had he not been stricken by cancer and was able to stay in the race until the end? On one hand he may have done less well than his brother who was not involved in his substance abuse scandals although he was constantly criticized as being an enabler. Although this might be true in a sense, the brothers were not as close as many perceived them to be. To Ford supporters, Doug did not hang around Rob when he used drugs and alcohol and Doug's defense of his brother was because he actually believed Rob's initial denials of using crack. It is possible Doug would have received more votes than Rob would have because of this.

However it is more likely Rob would have done better than his brother. Doug does not have Rob's charisma, personality and likeability. Rob was the one that would hand out his cellphone number and personally return calls not only of his constituents but any Torontonian outside of Ward 2 when he served as councillor. It was Rob who would meet constituents on their turf including those who lived in subsidized housing when they had a problem. Part of his problems arose as a result of his willingness to meet with residents in areas where gang members and drug dealers lived, the type of people most elected officials wouldn't go near with a 10-foot pole. It was Rob's ability to talk with anyone that made him appear as just a regular guy rather than a politician. To some, their loyalty to Rob was cult-like. It is possible had Rob been physically able to remain in the mayor's race, he would have obtained more votes than Doug received.

One thing is certain; people who consider themselves members of Ford Nation support both Rob and Doug. The brothers have the same views on issues, particularly when it comes to taxes, spending, government waste and subways.

There was always a divide between the downtown area and the suburbs. Although this is a generalization, the downtown core is seen as the home of the elites; people who are left wing in their thinking and who would support political candidates such as Chow. If not Chow then certainly someone who is a liberal or is seen to be more liberal in their thinking such as Tory. Downtowners are perceived to be mainly white, affluent, and not simply reliant on public transit but to whom the subways and connecting subways and buses are a favoured mode of transportation, at least for them.

The suburbs on the other hand are where many lower income people reside. The former cities of Scarborough and North York are home to many immigrants and first generation Canadians. These are the people who go to Timmy's for a double double rather than sip lattés at Starbucks. Many cannot afford to own and operate vehicles and are dependent upon public transit that necessitates taking one or more buses to reach a subway station in order to go downtown. A lot of these residents feel excluded when a mayor such as Miller pushed what is essentially a downtown agenda.

Although there has always been this divide, it became politically relevant after the one borough and five cities that formed the old Municipality of Metropolitan Toronto amalgamated in 1998. The merger resulted in the largest electoral district in Canada.

Although Rob has taken credit for this, the record for the most votes belongs to Mel Lastman, the former North York councillor and mayor who preceded Miller and was the first mayor of the new megacity. No major candidate ran against Lastman when he sought re-election in 2000 and he obtained almost 80% of the vote. As Canadians do not vote for prime minister or their provincial premier but only for the federal or provincial MP or MPP in their riding, the 483,000 plus votes Lastman got were the most votes ever obtained by a politician in a single election in the history of Canada.

Voters in 2014 did not strictly adhere to the downtown vs. suburbs. Tory managed to win wards in the south of Etobicoke, one in south Scarborough and in the north central part of North York. Nonetheless the generalities between the suburbs and downtown or between Ford and Tory/Chow voters managed to hold.

The elite media would never use the word "elite" to describe downtown residents. To elites, people who live downtown are simply "normal". Those who live in Etobicoke and Scarborough were described as low income and uneducated. Low income people were mocked for going against their own self-interest by supporting the Ford brothers rather that voting for someone like Chow who would feed their children and use other peoples' money to give them whatever they needed and wanted. In areas such as the Rexdale areas of Etobicoke there is a lot of Toronto housing that are hotbeds for drugs and gangs. The media made it appear that only the uneducated criminal class would support the Fords or at least Rob.

For example, the crack video was allegedly shot in Rexdale as was the still picture showing Rob holding a pipe with accompanied by young black men. Large buildings on Dixon Road, an area known as "Little Mogadishu," is home to one of the greatest concentration of Somalis outside of Somalia. These buildings were the epicentre of the police raids conducted during Project Traveller.

The media went out of their way to imply that these gang members were typical of those who supported the Fords. The oh so politically correct *Toronto Star* that is always ranting racism is everywhere and that has temper tantrums when anyone associates race with crime, went out of its way to describe the people who were with Rob when he smoked crack, not as drug dealers but as "Somali" drug dealers. This stopped after members of Toronto's Somali community complained. The rules of political correctness went out the window to achieve the greater goal of getting rid of the Fords.

The bottom line is that Ford supporters, implicitly or explicitly, were described in the media as non-whites who had low incomes and were not very bright. It was the type of stereotyping that the elite media abhors. Obviously, an exception is made when they do it.

Yet over 330,000 voters voted for Doug. That is a significant amount of people and cannot be explained by simply saying all these people are dumb, uneducated poor people who just do not know any better. There must be reasons why, despite the scandals involving the use of crack cocaine, being drunk in public, allegations of using prostitutes, getting into physical fights with staff, allegations of conflicts of interest and other council improprieties, making racist, homophobic, and anti-Semitic comments, being perceived as homophobic for not attending pride festivities, calling the Toronto police chief a "c**ks****r," hanging around with gang members and criminals and his confrontations with the media, such a large number of people chose to support Rob and later Doug over his rivals in the election.

The Fords were certainly the political opposites of Chow. It is difficult to imagine that well informed Chow supporters would ever vote for the Fords even if they were scandal-free. And no fiscally conservative Toronto resident would ever vote for the socialist Chow. John Tory was the wild card in all this. To those who lean to the right, he was seen as a conservative although he is a Red Tory. And to those who lean left, he was the perfect "Anybody But Ford" candidate. That explains his win but does not explain why so many people stuck with the Ford brothers. But members of Ford Nation had their reasons and the supporters of Ford cannot be simply written off as uneducated, low income knuckle-draggers who admire someone who smokes crack and hangs around with drug dealers.

Chapter 7

Members of Ford Nation

So who are these people who comprise what is known as Ford Nation? Well, it is certainly true some are those that were stereotyped by the media such as the *Toronto Star*; low income people with not much education. What the media means by this is a typical Ford supporter is likely an immigrant or second generation Canadian living in subsidized housing. This group does include drug dealers, gangbangers and people who, unlike the elites in the downtown area, are primarily not white. These people are so dumb that in casting their votes for a Ford, they are acting against their best interests. Ideally they should vote for Chow or someone like her who will tax the evil rich and provide them with everything they need as the city of Toronto is marches towards utopia.

The main reason these people supported the Fords was because Rob showed he cared about them. If they had a problem, he would visit them where they live and do what he could to help them. While many politicians champion the issues important to lower income people, they do not spend any time hanging around with them. Rob and Doug, despite their wealth were not downtowners whose major concerns were the number of bicycle lanes in the city and making the subway less crowded. The fact that Doug campaigned for mayor for only six weeks of the 10-month campaign and obtained almost a third of a million votes leads to the conclusion that support for the Fords is a lot broader than just those who live in the depressed suburban areas of Rexdale and Scarborough.

The prominence of cell phones and social media played a large part both in attempts to bring the Fords down and in the support of the brothers. Anything Rob did in public was photographed or videoed and sent to the anti-Ford media who played in on their websites and provided pictures in their print publications. There was nothing too small to attempt to embarrass their hated mayor such as Rob walking out of a KFC with food while he was supposedly on a diet or leaving a liquor store with a purchase, acts engaged in by ordinary people every day. There were also videos and stills of Rob being drunk getting into a cab at city hall or on the street at the Taste of the Danforth. And there was also the video of Rob at the Steak Queen, calling Toronto's police chief a "c**ks****r" and speaking Jamaican patois. Various recordings were made of Rob making racist comments, referring to various groups of people as n*****s, kikes and fags.

Then there was the crack scandal. Although the original alleged crack video has never been released to the media or the public, a still picture was publicized by the media showing Rob allegedly smoking crack with some "black guys," one of those who was murdered shortly thereafter. And there was a portion of another video showing Rob appearing to be smoking crack in what was said to be his sister's basement. There was a video released showing Rob ranting and raving and threatening to kill an unnamed person.

Just as technology was used to attempt to bring the Fords down, it was also used to permit their supporters to form a cohesive group. Given that all of the major media turned against not only Rob but Doug as well during the 2014 campaign, it is highly unlikely Rob and Doug, particularly Doug, would have done as well as they did had it not been for social media. Positive things the Fords did, and yes there were many of these that were basically ignored by the Ford-hating mainstream media, were reported on social media sites. Social media also allowed members of Ford Nation a place to go to meet and have discussions with likeminded people.

The most prominent of these social media sites, although there are others is the Facebook page, *I Hate the War on Mayor Rob Ford*. The

IHTWOMRF page was created towards the end of 2011, about a year and a half before the crack scandal that attracted the attention of the world. The page remains active even after the 2014 election and has over 4,200 "likes" at the beginning of 2015. The members of this page and other pro-Ford social media sites like to show people who support Rob and Doug are not the dummies portrayed in the anti-Ford mainstream media.

The IHTWOMRF page was begun by Neil Flagg. Flagg, like many small "c" conservatives grew up as a liberal in a liberal part of Toronto. He says he was never really comfortable with the liberal mindset and in university, he became a conservative. This happened during the early 1990s when the Reform Party began to make its mark on the Canadian political scene. At the time, Flagg was studying journalism at the University of Western Ontario.

In 1998, Flagg began his own business, Sports Poster Warehouse, a business he still runs today. Many of his customers and business contacts are American and he realized those who are conservative, especially the ones that live in the American heartland, are not the dumb racist rubes they are often portrayed to be in the media. They struck him by and large as kind, polite, open minded and happy. The more contact he had with these Americans the more small government, independent and family oriented conservative he became.

During the 2000 US election, Flagg was able to tune into the *Fox News* channel and noticed the American situation was portrayed differently on that network than in the rest of the mainstream media. He learned a lot of Americans were fed up with Bill Clinton's lying and cheating and the election was not going to be the cakewalk for Al Gore that the liberal media said it would be.

During the 2008 election, Flagg became a Sarah Palin fan and watched how the liberal media attempted to destroy her and eventually forced her to resign from the office of governor of Alaska with their distortions, lies and set-ups. When the Republican convention to nominate candidates for the 2012 campaign took place, he noticed how not only the mainstream media but the Republican establishment worked to destroy her.

A little over a year into Rob's term as mayor, Flagg noticed that Rob was receiving the same treatment Palin was given south of the border. If he wasn't being sued for one thing or another, he was being laughed at because of his weight. In October 2011, Flagg, along with his friend Sue Ferguson-Ross began the Facebook page.

The first major event that took place around the time the page was begun was the "Marg Delahunty" incident. "Marg Delahunty" is a character played by alleged comedian Mary Walsh on the long running *CBC* show, *This Hour has 22 Minutes*. Part of Walsh's shtick is to ambush famous people and ask them questions. As she often did, when she approached Ford, she was wearing her warrior princess outfit.

Although Walsh ambushes politicians and others in public places, she showed up at Ford's home at 8 a.m. while he was getting into his car. Although Walsh denies this, Ford said his five-year-old daughter was with him, got scared and ran back into the house. Ford followed his daughter to his home and then called 911.

Walsh saw nothing wrong with going to the mayor's home early in the morning rather than doing what she usually does in public. Ford, who has had his share of threats, believed Walsh and the person with her were trying to get into his car. He said he did not know who she was. To the Ford-hating elites, it was unbelievable that someone would not faithfully watch the *CBC* show and know who Walsh and her Delahunty character were.

At city hall later that day, Ford said he has no problem with what Walsh does but said going to his home at 8 a.m. when his children were there crossed the line. The media however made fun of him for not realizing (or lying about) what had happened. The police took no action.

Following every incident involving some wrongdoing or alleged wrongdoing on the part of the mayor, the number of people who frequented the IHTWOMRF page and joined in the discussions increased. By the time the crack scandal broke out, the page was the place for the defenders of the mayor to go.

Contrary to conventional wisdom, many members of Ford Nation are like Flagg. They are university educated, have families with small children, have homes with mortgages and run their own businesses. They resent the constant increases in their property taxes and new taxes such as the hated $60 vehicle registration tax brought in by Miller. And they don't want their tax money spent in the United Kingdom to fight climate change. These fiscal conservatives are equally upset about the scandal-plagued Ontario government that wastes billions of their tax dollars either due to sheer incompetence or for pure political gain such as the cancellation of the two gas plants during the 2011 provincial election.

Those on the left who either have jobs or live off the state resent "the rich." This became extremely popular after the 2008 election of Barack Obama who spent much of his early days in the Oval Office demonizing "the rich." To these people, anyone like Flagg who has their own business is of course rich. As anyone who is or has run their own small business knows this is hardly the case. Many Ford supporters who have their own businesses have to struggle to make a living. This is especially true when the economy is bad as it was after the economic downturn in 2008.

How "the rich" are viewed by many on the left was illustrated by something that happened at the beginning of the 2014 Toronto municipal election campaign. In order to show she was not rich like the Fords and Tory, candidate Karen Stintz put out a statement that she wasn't like her rivals—she was just an ordinary soccer mom working to pay the mortgage. She tweeted, "I am just like you. I have a mortgage, kids, one car and soccer games. Let's make it better."

People immediately took to social media to criticize the candidate. They pointed out how they didn't have a car or couldn't afford a house or get a mortgage or did not have the money so their children could play organized soccer. Of course the reality is there are thousands of people in Toronto like Stintz and like the employed members of Ford Nation. They have to work hard in bad economic times to be able to pay the mortgage and to afford the amenities Stintz spoke about.

Even if members of Ford Nation could use a little help to improve their financial positions, they do not look to government to give it to them. All they want is to be able to take care of themselves without governments increasing their taxes to pay for pie-in-the-sky ideas such as greening the planet or to provide luxurious lifestyles to politicians and their friends. Members of Ford Nation live in a world where if they go out and buy some plants they water them themselves.

Unlike those on the left, members of Ford Nation are not jealous because Ford has more wealth than many of them do. They admire the Fords for paying their own way when they could properly bill them, the taxpayers. And they like the fact the brothers, because they are not dependent upon the largesse of unions, corporations or other special interest groups, can put the welfare of ordinary people like them first.

One urban myth is that conservative politicians do not appeal to women. This is especially true when these politicians are like the Fords who are loud, outspoken, often crude and prone to making politically incorrect utterances. Contrary to this notion, many members of Ford Nation are women and according to Flagg, they are some of the brothers' most ardent defenders. He attributes this to the fact that, unlike many men today, both Rob and Doug are alpha males. They say and do what they want and are seemingly oblivious to the fact others, such as the mainstream media, constantly criticize them. This is in sharp contrast to a society in which many men, including politicians, strive to show their feminine side.

Many Ford-haters and some in the mainstream media have characterized members of Ford Nation as being members of a cult. As in any large group there are some who go to extremes such as the woman who got hysterical when the 2014 election results were announced and likened newly elected mayor John Tory to a member of ISIS. And yes, there are some people who believed every word Rob said when he lied about such things as his crack use and his drunken appearance at the hockey game at the ACC while he was a councillor. Some today refuse to believe the crack video exists and will not believe it is real until they actually see it. If the video does not in fact exist and its existence was simply made up to make trouble for Rob, there would have to be a conspiracy between reporters Doolittle and Donovan, Toronto Police Chief Bill Blair, Ontario Superior Court Justice Ian Nordheimer and various members of the Toronto Police

Service, the Ontario courts and the *Toronto Star*. While some may have a cult-like attraction to the Fords, the vast majority of people who comprise Ford Nation have cogent arguments why they want to see a Ford in charge of the city of Toronto. Disagreeing with these reasons does not make Ford Nation a cult.

And there is one more thing that members of Ford Nation by and large have in common. This has to do with their views on the mainstream liberal media.

Chapter 8

The Media

Another thing a lot of members of Ford Nation have in common is they listen to US talk radio, watch *Fox News* and read conservative publications on the Internet. Canada of course has talk radio in the sense there are stations where hosts talk rather than play music and people call in to express their views, but none of these programs approach those of Rush Limbaugh, Mark Levin, Sean Hannity, Glenn Beck and others. While Canada's constitution contains the right of free speech, this right in limited compared to the United States. In February 2013, the Supreme Court of Canada upheld the provincial and federal human rights commissions as reasonable limits on the enshrined right to freedom of expression. The court determined this limitation on freedom of expression is an appropriate balance to other societal values such as respect for groups with specific identities and the dignity that is inherent to all human beings. Although the most offending section of the federal legislation that effectively banned "hate speech" on the Internet was repealed six months later, the reality of human rights commissions and the Canadian Radio and Television Commission (CRTC) that regulates commercial airwaves effectively prohibits some of the speech heard south of the border. Like the Fords and the integrity commissioner, radio hosts would be forever dragged before human rights tribunals if their shows approached anything that is heard on American talk radio.

The myriad of conservative talk radio and other media in the United States illustrates the deficiency of the so-called mainstream media. Progressive critics of US talk radio take the juvenile position that people like Limbaugh and the others are simply making things up. They are lying. These accusations are often made by people who never listen to these programs but instead rely on what is said on *Media Matters* and similar left wing sites as well as the mainstream media.

Listening to and watching American conservative media shows the mainstream media is biased and often conceals facts in order to make what they are reporting appear the way they want to. There are numerous examples of this but the following two will serve as examples of this happening. After the Affordable Care Act (Obamacare) became law in 2010, Obama said several times that if people liked their doctor or liked their current insurance plan they could keep them. Conservative commentators constantly said the ACA could not possibly work if people could keep their current choices. They were called racist. In 2014, it became obvious this was not the case and the White House and their sycophants in the mainstream media could not ignore these facts any longer. Unlike those in the mainstream media who simply parroted the administration's talking points, the view that people could not retain their own doctors and insurance plans came from researchers in conservative think tanks who, unlike Nancy Pelosi, had actually read the legislation.

A recent and perhaps one of the most egregious example of media manipulation concerns the decision of the grand jury in Ferguson, Missouri not to indict police officer Darren Wilson in the shooting death of Michael Brown in the summer of 2014. The mainstream media adopted the mantra of the protesters after the grand jury decision of "Hands up. Don't shoot." Even some on air CNN personalities held up their hands and said "don't shoot." This chant was based upon the assumption that Wilson shot Brown after he indicated he was surrendering by holding his hands up and yelling "don't shoot." The media loves stories that pits blacks and other minorities as victims of whites, especially white cops who are perceived as racist. To them, Wilson was a cop who got up that summer morning and decided to go hunting for blacks.

What the mainstream media did in their portrayal of the "Gentle Giant" or "child" as Brown was sometimes referred to, was to totally ignore the evidence that was placed before the grand jury. It is true a witness had said Brown was surrendering when he was shot. But other witnesses, some of them black, testified Brown was charging at Wilson and refused commands to stop when he was shot. This version confirmed Wilson's account of the event and was also consistent with the forensic evidence placed before the grand jury. The forensic evidence also confirmed Wilson's account that Brown had previously attempted to get his gun. But it was a much better story to say Brown was shot because he was black.

Conservative publications and talk radio did not attempt to do what the mainstream media did; that is to cheer Obama while ignoring any problems inherent in the Affordable Care Act and disregard the evidence showing Brown was anything other than a young black man shot to death without justification. Those who read conservative media and listen to talk radio were able to get the truth.

The critics of conservative media, as indicated earlier, many who never bother reading or listening to it, concluded these right wing whackos like Rush Limbaugh and Sean Hannity are simply lying. When Limbaugh, who is credited with saving AM radio at a time when music stations were going over to FM, began his syndicated show in 1988 it was easy to simply call him a liar. But we are now in another century.

The truth the mainstream media attempts to suppress is not only reported on by conservative websites and radio programs but the information is available on the Internet. Regarding the ACA, some conservatives actually read the legislation and concluded it could not work if everyone was allowed to keep their then current plans and doctors. The legislation is available on the net to anyone who wants to go through it. And the evidence before the Ferguson grand jury is also available in the Internet. Instead of taking Limbaugh's or Hannity's word for it, anyone who was interested in learning the truth can read both the ACA and the evidence before the Ferguson grand jury.

People who scoff at social media and only watch *CNN* or *CBC* never see the other side of the story. Those who follow conservative media are able to see both sides of the issue because like it or not, they are inundated with what the mainstream media is reporting.

Those who listen or read conservative media understand the bias in the mainstream media and members of Ford Nation who listen to US talk radio have learned to be skeptical of what the mainstream media was telling them about the Fords.

Many people know nothing about media bias or claim it does not exist. These are people who only listen to, read, and watch mainstream media sources that usually report the same facts and the same point of view. To those who restrict themselves to such sources, the mainstream media is seen as reporting "facts" and since the consumers are unaware of anything other than what these sources tell them, they become simply the facts. Anyone who disagrees with these facts is seen as having a political reason for rejecting what is obviously the truth. But bias in the media always exists, at least at some level and it can occur in both progressive and conservative news sources.

Some believe bias in the media can only occur if the source reports facts that are obviously untrue. In the case of Rob, both *Gawker* and the *Toronto Star* reported about the existence of the video appearing to show the mayor smoking crack cocaine. As time went by this video was confirmed by Toronto's police chief who said the video had been recovered and it was substantially as reported by the media. Despite this fact, some Rob fans refuse to accept the fact the video exists despite not only the confirmation of it by Bill Blair but the fact the video was the subject of court proceedings. But most people accepted the fact of its existence, especially after Rob admitted he did in fact smoke crack.

To many, this constituted proof the media was not biased. They reported on a video and its existence was confirmed, therefore the sources that reported on it were not biased. But there is more to media bias than whether or not what is reported is true or is eventually found to be true.

The way the media highlights certain stories can indicate bias. Scandals involving Rob were always front page news whereas when a good Liberal such as former London, Ontario mayor Joe Fontana was accused and later convicted of fraud, it was reported but rarely made headlines. And the frequency of coverage of one high profile person over another can also indicate bias. A good example of this is the coverage of Ben Levin. Levin was a provincial civil servant who served for a time as the deputy minister of education. He was deputy minister when a controversial sex education program that would have taught Grade 3 students about homosexuality, Grade 6 students about masturbation and Grade 7 students about oral and anal sex was in the process of being introduced. In 2010 as a result of protests by social conservatives, McGuinty withdrew the program. It will be reintroduced under McGuinty's successor, Kathleen Wynne.

In July 2013, Levin was charged with making and distributing child pornography, counselling to commit an indictable offence and arranging to commit a sexual offence upon a child under the age of 16 years. Two additional child pornography charges were laid after Levin's initial arrest.

During the latter part of 2014, Levin, who is out on bail, made a couple of court appearances. Other than one reporter from *Sun News Network*, the media was not present. Levin was close to Premier Wynne and served as a member of her transition team. At the time of this writing, Levin has not been tried and is presumed to be innocent. But the vast majority of the mainstream media has shown no interest in the fact a man who was close to Wynne and was the deputy education minister at the time a controversial sex education program was rolled out, might have an illegal sexual interest in small children. It wasn't worth sending reporters to court for. Given his position in the Ministry of Education, it was no big deal. More reporters were sent to Gravenhurst, Ontario to see Rob's car in an impound lot. Levin got a lot less coverage than Rob did when he announced he was going to lose weight and then was spotted leaving a KFC restaurant.

The major media bias exists regarding Rob because he was put under a lot more scrutiny than other elected officials. Perhaps the classic example of this type of bias was what happened during and after the 2008 US presidential elections.

Shortly after Barack Obama's victory, Tom Brokaw appeared on *PBS* with Charlie Rose. Both men discussed the fact that no one, particularly the two newsmen knew very much about the man who was just elected president of the United States. They discussed that they didn't know anything about his views on foreign policy, about what books he reads or about who his heroes are. They knew nothing about him.

Neither Brokaw nor Rose thought it was strange that their profession, journalism, was the one that should have gone out and discovered Obama's background so people could be informed about a man who might be elected president of the United States. Whenever this question did arise, the media would plead poverty; they just didn't have the money to send reporters to Chicago and elsewhere to check up on Obama. In another irony, they seemed to have enough funds to send reporters to Alaska to go through Sarah Palin's garbage.

The mainstream media hated the Fords. As a result, the brothers were put under more scrutiny than not only the candidates who ran against them but others who were seeking elected office. And anything that happened to the Fords was big news, deserving of constant repetition. The media was successful in demonizing them.

A classic example of treating the Fords differently than other politicians is the way the media constantly made fun of Rob because he obviously had substance abuse problems. The hypocrisy of the left, including the left wing media, was nicely illustrated by an article that appeared in *The American Prospect* magazine, a prominent US progressive magazine. Written by the online editor, Clare Malone, it was published on November 8, 2013, about a week after Blair announced the crack video does exist and was recovered by police.

After expressing surprise that Ontario law didn't provide for throwing Rob out of office, Malone went on to write about how progressives fought to have alcoholism and drug addiction treated as medical problems. She concluded, quite rightly, that the Toronto mayor had a substance abuse problem that should be treated as an illness. Yet she found society had regressed; people laughed at the videos showing Rob almost falling down in his drunken stupors. He was viewed as the stereotypical "lush" who was funny to watch.

Malone's description of how Rob was when he was high or drunk was exactly the way he was treated by the media. They laughed at him and made jokes about him in between the odd statement he should seek help. If he had been a good liberal politician there was no way he would ever have been laughed at. He would have been treated the way Malone expects progressives to treat someone who has an addiction.

The word "bullying" is used quite a bit these days. The media loved to say how Doug in particular was a bully. When he accused the Toronto police chief of carrying out a criminal investigation of his brother Doug was called a bully. While bullying is a serious societal problem, especially with young people on the Internet, it was ludicrous to think Doug's accusations against a six-foot plus cop constituted bullying.

If that act is to be included what constitutes bullying, then there is no doubt the media bullied Rob. Besides making fun of him for his addiction problems, they hounded him. Reporters constantly tried to get him to admit he was a crack addict although he denied it. For anyone else, the denials would be seen as part of the illness. But there was so much hate for the uncouth conservative who was not like them, they "regressed" as Malone would put it.

The media, particularly Mary Walsh and Daniel Dale, had no compunction about going to Rob's house early in the evening or early in the morning to hound him. They would never, ever treat a left wing politician that way. There are a lot of unanswered questions concerning the provincial government scandals that cost taxpayers billions of dollars. But the media would never have gone to McGuinty or Wynne's homes to demand answers. Despite the Liberal government corruption, they are the good guys. Rob deserved what he got. Members of Ford Nation saw the actions of progressives towards the Fords as acts of bullying.

The following are three examples of the media going well beyond simply reporting the news and creating deliberate hit pieces against the man who in their opinion, was simply unfit to be mayor because of his conservatism and because he was, for lack of a better term, not one of them.

One already mentioned above was the hit piece just before the 2010 election when the *Globe and Mail* published a piece by Stephen Marche wherein he used the word "fat" 17 times in describing Ford. The problem was no so much with Marche as it was with the editors who thought it was perfectly okay to make fun of someone's obesity in the pages of the publication that bills itself as "Canada's National Newspaper."

Rob was not the first elected official who is obese or who has a weight problem. Former Liberal MP and MPP Elinor Caplan comes to mind. But does anyone seriously think the left wing *Globe* would have made fun of a liberal politician's weight? Of course not. But Rob was a conservative and besides he was crude and refused to be politically correct. It was fair game to make fun of his appearance.

As bad as this article was, it paled in comparison to an article that appeared in *Toronto Life*. *Toronto Life* is a glossy monthly magazine that serves the elites in the city. After the Fords supposedly referred to their family as the "Canadian Kennedys," Steve Kupferman wrote an article entitled, *The Ford Family Tree*. The entire Ford Family was shown in family tree form with little blurbs about each one.

It seems important to Ford haters to highlight the fact some members of the family who have never been involved in elected politics are or were involved in drugs. If that wasn't bad enough, even young children were shown on the Ford family tree, including Rob's young children who were nine and five at the time the article was published.

Underneath the title were the words, "They call themselves the 'Canadian Kennedys.' You be the judge." Besides picking on all members of the Ford family and bringing small children into it, this has to be one of the worst pieces of journalism ever to be published.

The writer invites people to compare the two families but there is absolutely nothing in the article about the Kennedys. When speaking about

Doug Sr., the Ford family patriarch, Kupferman sarcastically writes he "advocated for—Surprise!—tax cuts and fiscal responsibility..." Kupferman either doesn't know or doesn't care that John F. Kennedy advocated for tax cuts while president.

A year before his death, JFK spoke at the Economic Club of New York where he said that high tax rates that kept the economy from overheating after World War II was now acting as a drag on the economy and taxes should be reduced. Three months after his death Lyndon Johnson got the tax cuts through Congress. Top marginal rates were reduced from 91% to 70% while the lowest rate was cut from 20% to 14%. Yet the writer of the *Toronto Life* piece doesn't't mention JFK and tax cuts at all. Cutting taxes was only used in the article to take a shot at Rob and Doug's late father.

What was also missing from the magazine article was any mention of others in the Kennedy family. While the magazine gloated over the fact that some members of the Ford family were involved with drugs or arrested for various criminal acts, *Toronto Life* made no references to any members of the Kennedy family other than the late president.

A lot of the Kennedys used drugs and some died young. Robert Kennedy Jr., a darling of the downtown elites who love to peruse *Toronto Life*, was arrested and convicted of possession of heroin. Bobby Jr., like his uncle JFK and his grandfather Joe Kennedy, was also a noted philanderer. Ethel Kennedy's nephew, Michael Skakel, was convicted of murder in the 1975 death of 15-year-old Martha Moxely. And then there's Ted Kennedy who drove off a bridge in Edgartown, Massachusetts in 1969 and then fled the scene leaving his passenger, Mary Jo Kopechne, 28, in the car to drown. Paraphrasing John Connolly, the late governor of Texas, at least the Fords "never drowned nobody."

So Kupferman asks his readers to compare the two families but gives no details about the Kennedys, hoping the readers will rely on the myth they were simply a wholesome family who inhabited Camelot. What purports to be an article about the two families was just a cover to make fun of the Fords. Readers were asked to compare apples and oranges with not a word about the latter fruit.

But at least *Toronto Life* doesn't purport to be a news organization and its readers buy the publication to look at glossy pictures of the who's who in Toronto, find the latest openings of trendy restaurants and seek recommendations for fine wine. It's likely the magazine's readers would laugh at the Fords and would not have the least interest in the problems including drug use of the Kennedys. It was a hit piece pure and simple.

The *Toronto Star* on the other hand is a real newspaper and it is hard to believe that any news media that at least pretends to be an unbiased news source would publish the following. This story began in early December 2013, when John Honderich was chairman of the board of Torstar that owns the *Toronto Star*. For 10 years between 1994 and 2004, Honderich was the publisher of the newspaper, a job previously held by his father, Bleland. Honderich editorialized about what he called the "deafening silence" of community leaders about Rob's use of crack cocaine and other scandals. Honderich could not believe these so-called leaders were refraining from doing what he was doing, calling for the mayor to resign before his term ended. The fact that prominent citizens were not speaking out against the city's mayor at the height of the crack scandal was a perfectly proper subject for an editorial. But Honderich did not stop there.

Following the column, Honderich sent letters to 70 people he identified as civic leaders, asking them if they thought Ford was fit to continue in office given the scandals. In what Conrad Black, writing in the *National Post* described as "ideological blackmail," the letter said if recipients did not want Ford gone, Honderich wanted to know why. And if a civic leader did not reply to the letter, that fact would be noted in the *Star*.

In early January, just as the formal 2014 campaign began, the *Toronto Star* published the results of the replies or non-replies of these civic leaders. The article was written not by Honderich but by one of his flunky reporters, Marco Chown Oved. The upshot was no one chose to publicly defend the mayor but 21 of the recipients declined to be shaken down into commenting. As promised, those who declined comment were named in the article.

The three above incidents; the use of the word "fat" to describe the mayor, the comparison of the Fords to the Kennedys without giving any facts about the latter family, and Honderich's telling civic leaders to speak out or else are but three examples of how the media went to extreme lengths to attack the mayor. While the media obviously affected many Torontonians and this may have cost Doug's election as mayor, nothing the left wing media did dissuaded members of Ford Nation as seeing Rob and Doug as the only logical choices to lead Toronto.

Chapter 9

The Fords – True Fiscal Conservatives

As difficult as it is for many people to believe, there are a lot of small "c" conservatives in Canada. While social conservatism is not all that common in a country that has legalized same sex marriage and since the late 1980s has had no law whatsoever concerning abortion, the last two municipal elections have shown there is no shortage of fiscal conservatives in Toronto, a city that usually votes Liberal or NDP both federally and provincially.

The main attraction of the Fords to their supporters known as Ford Nation is their fiscal conservatism. Their desire not to waste taxpayers' money almost borders on an obsession.

Fiscal conservatism, like many other things these days is relative. If a liberal politician wants to spend $1 billion to open a widget factory and a conservative politician criticizes it, saying the factory can be opened for $800,000, the latter is seen as being a fiscal conservative. But a real fiscal conservative would first question the need for the widget factory in the first place. Will the benefits of the factory in terms of employment and trade outweigh the cost? These types of questions are rarely asked.

A real life example of this occurred in Ontario in 2010. Then Premier Dalton McGuinty announced his government was going to spend $20 million over four years to give 75 foreign students scholarships to study in the province. The leader of the Progressive Conservatives at the time was Tim Hudak.

Hudak could hardly be described as a tax and spender. He was the one, who, to the surprise of even his candidates, announced during the first week of the 2014 election campaign that he would get rid of 100,000 provincial civil servants. Had he been elected to lead the province and been able to do this, there is no doubt that not only would the taxpayers have saved money but the size of government would have been reduced. It was a conservative's dream. As indicted above, Hudak appeared to enjoy the thought of firing people just because there were too many of them and this cost him the election.

When McGuinty made his announcement about the scholarships, Hudak's knee jerk reaction was to say the money should be spent on Ontario students not students in other countries. This is not true fiscal conservatism. The question should have been whether it was necessary to spend $20 million on students, either those already in Ontario or those from other countries. Would there have been a benefit to Ontario by giving these scholarships to foreign students? Would there have been more or less benefit to the province if the money was spent on Ontario students? Was there a need to spend the $20 million at all? Were there other things the province could have spent $20 million on that would have provided greater benefits to the taxpayers than the scholarships would?

McGuinty was "spend, spend, spend," while on this issue Hudak wanted to "spend, spend, spend," on other things. It was like the old joke about simply haggling over the price. Except with McGuinty and Hudak, the price was the same.

It is impossible to believe the Fords, in the same position would have agreed to spend $20 million on something just because it sounded better than what the premier wanted to spend it on.

Much of Rob Ford's attraction to the members of Ford Nation is his concern about the billing of even the smallest expense to the taxpayer he thought was unnecessary. During the 2010 campaign, Ford mentioned one item he had been angry about since he was first elected to council 10 years before—the cost of watering plants at city hall.

Back in 2010 the city of Toronto was spending about $77,000 a year for unionized workers to water plants throughout city hall. But not all plants. The employee would first check to make sure the plant was one owned by the municipal government. If the plant was one brought into city hall by an employee then it was up to the plant's owner to water it. It probably took more time to determine the plant's ownership than it did to water it. Ford thought this was nonsensical and he was not alone.

Back in 2007, Ford put a motion forward to take the cost of watering plants out of the city budget. The motion was defeated by a vote of 30-13 and the councillor was laughed at for making the motion in the first place. Being laughed at was not an unusual event when Rob tried to save even a little public money. Later during the mayoral campaign that saw him obtain 47% of the vote, Ford said the amount of money the city spends was the number one issue of those he met while campaigning. And he was right.

With operating and capital budgets in the billions of dollars, the saving of $77,000 paid to water city hall owned plants would not have made a difference. But Ford supporters knew that a person who saved them pocket change by cutting small expenses would not waste their money on major expenditures. Unlike other politicians who freely spend money on corporate interests, unions, and a variety of special interest groups, Ford's main concern was with the ordinary taxpayer. For those who agreed with Ford that the city has a spending problem, not a revenue problem, this was a refreshing change.

Ford never came across like a typical politician and even some of his supporters thought it was funny when he announced he would seek to lead the city of Toronto in 2010. Often referred to as a buffoon, Ford's fiscal conservatism would not have had the appeal it did were the economy booming and all levels of government had been restrained in their spending. But this was far from the case.

While Canada was not hit as hard as other countries such as the United States in the financial meltdown that occurred in 2008, Canadians were affected. Contrary to media reports, many of Ford's supporters are small business people struggling to keep afloat during what has been called the worst economy since the Great Depression. Not wasting their hard earned money on such things as watering plants at city hall had more appeal in these bad economic times than they would have if everything had been rosy.

Worried about their businesses and jobs, Torontonians were not in the mood to see their property taxes increasing above the rate of inflation and being subjected to new taxes such as the Vehicle Registration Tax and the municipal Land Transfer Tax. And these same people did not want to see these new and higher taxes wasted on such things as an office in the UK set up to save the world from global warming. As these residents were falling behind during the Miller administration, their mayor was using their money to cave into the city's unions.

Ford perhaps would never have become mayor if Toronto had been located in any province other than Ontario. The provincial Liberals had been in power since 2003 and the party began with the promise by then leader Dalton McGuinty that Ontarians would not pay one cent more in taxes than they were then paying under the PC government if they brought his party to power. As soon as the Liberals were elected with a majority, McGuinty imposed a health tax, the largest tax increase in the province's history.

The way McGuinty handled what was described as his out and out lie, illustrates how someone who was a fiscal conservative could look comparatively better to those who feel they are being squeezed at every turn. McGuinty denied the tax was a tax. He said don't be silly; it's not a tax it's a health premium.

Years ago, Ontario did in fact have a health premium residents were required to pay in order to be eligible for government health care. Contracts the provincial government had with its unions contained a clause that the employer (the government) was responsible for payment of the premiums. Despite the fact these premiums were long gone, the clause was never removed in some of the unions' collective agreements. Civil servants who were members of those unions jumped for joy because they would not be responsible for paying this premium; their employer the government would.

McGuinty told them not to be silly, it was a tax, not a premium. The matter was eventually settled by a court that ruled it was in fact a tax. McGuinty and his government treated the taxpayers of Ontario as idiots. This made a lot of people ready for Ford's message of respect for taxpayers.

In Canada, the federal government has an equalization program, that in effect transfers money from the country's well off provinces to the poorer ones. The theory of this equalization is so each province will be able to provide the same level of services for all Canadians. For the first time, in 2009/10, Ontario went from being a "have" province to a "have-not" and this was a direct result of high taxes and the wasteful spending of the Liberal government. Newfoundland and Labrador, the perennial have-not province whose residents have been the brunt of "Newfie" jokes, became a have province around the same time. Residents of Newfoundland and Labrador now sit around in bars and tell Ontario jokes.

In what seems as an anomaly, the 2014 provincial election that saw the corrupt Wynne Liberals go from a minority to a majority government, the PCs were completely wiped out in the city of Toronto. The Liberals captured all but two downtown seats that were won by the NDP. The suburbs that voted overwhelmingly for Rob in 2010 and to a smaller extent for Doug in 2014, elected Liberal MPPs. But this says more about the state of the PC Party than it did about the desire of these voters to have a tax and spend government.

Rob and Doug are unusual politicians. Not because Rob used crack cocaine in some of his many drunken stupors, thousands of people do that, but because they were obsessed with not wasting even the smallest amount of tax money on what they saw as frivolous or unnecessary.

During the 2014 municipal election campaign, it was pointed out that John Tory's best chance of winning was to adopt the Fords' policies of fiscal conservatism and position himself as someone who would govern like Ford but without the scandals and without bringing what was often described as a circus to Toronto. Tory did not do so and won the election anyway but in the end it would not have been successful. Unlike the Ford brothers, Tory was perceived by many as willing to say and do anything to get elected. The reality was neither Tory nor any other candidate could have matched Rob and Doug's passion for stopping the gravy train and respect for the taxpayers. It was the passion rather than the just the policies that appealed to members of Ford Nation despite the scandals including Rob's admission he had smoked crack.

Chapter 10

'Ford Never Ripped Us Off'

Even in staid Canada, scandals involving elected politicians are not unknown. While there is the odd scandal involving sex and alcohol use, many of today's wrongdoing by the political class involves elected officials enriching themselves and their political friends at the expense of the taxpayers.

The Ford crack scandal was different than simply unacceptable behaviour. First, it involved crack, a drug usually associated with gang members and criminals, the kind of people the mayor of Canada's largest city seemed to spend a lot of time with.

The other difference is that when Ford used drugs or drank to excess, he did so in public or at least surrounded by people as was the case in the allegation he smoked crack while in the basement of his sister Kathy's home. He did it in public at a time technology was such that everyone has a cellphone capable of taking videos and still pictures. Had Ford been an elected official at a time before this advance in technology, there would have been a lot of gossip, whispering and speculation but no corroborating evidence of what he was doing. Some of the allegations, proved true or not, were the stuff movies are made about.

When scandals involve money, the wrongful act is usually done in private. Even if done in public it would involve the politician signing a false document and if a video of it were shown, it would be as exciting as watching paint dry.

Although Ford haters will give examples of Ford's use of city resources for his private interests, there is absolutely no evidence he or his brother Doug ever spent taxpayers' money to enrich themselves. Yes, Ford did use city staff to purchase vodka for him after cellphone videos had been taken of him walking out of a liquor store with a bottle, uploaded, and then reported on by the media. Ditto when he was publicly laughed at when shown leaving a KFC outlet with take-out food at a time when he was trying to lose weight.

And yes, he did spend time coaching high school football when it was arguable he should have been conducting city business. And there were allegations he was having his staff help him with his coaching duties. The kids he coached were low income teens, or as former Mayor Miller liked to refer to them, "disadvantaged youth." While Miller would occasionally invite some of these disadvantaged, mainly black young people down to city hall for a photo-op, he and other elites of the political class wouldn't be caught dead in their presence in the areas they lived in. Giving money to these disadvantaged youth was praised. Rob giving his time to them was criticized.

But the Ford brothers, as scandal-plagued as their tenure at city hall was, never improperly benefited financially from anything they did. Even the conflict of interest case that saw the mayor ordered out of office before the decision was reversed, involved $3,150 that everyone was agreed, did not go to Ford.

At the time Rob was both councillor and mayor, there seemed to be an abundance of scandals involving the proven facts and allegations of wasting the taxpayers' money coupled with outright criminal acts done by politicians to enrich themselves. These incidents happened both at the federal and provincial level. Coupled with the increasing and new taxes imposed by Rob's predecessor, the ripping off of taxpayers at the federal and provincial level gave impetus to his supporters for not only Rob's message of respect for taxpayers but to support a mayor who did not steal or waste their money. As a result of constantly feeling their tax dollars are always being wasted, members of Ford Nation were prepared to support their frugal mayor no matter what he did in his personal life. Had these financial scandals not occurred in such magnitude and frequency, support for the Fords would probably have been a lot lower.

Bev Oda was a federal Conservative cabinet minister and in 2012 she served as the International Co-operation Minister in the Harper government. She had travelled to London, England to attend a conference on, of all things, the immunization of poor children in third world countries. While the conference organizers had arranged hotel accommodations for the attendees, the hotel was not suitable for Queen Bev so she booked a room at the fashionable Savoy Hotel. The room cost twice the price of the original one, and she billed the excess to the Canadian taxpayers. While there she enjoyed, or at least hopefully enjoyed, a glass of orange juice that cost $16 that she dutifully charged to the taxpayers. Oda had gone through a similar experience in 2006 when she went to the Juno awards. Forgoing the minivan provided to take her to and from the event, she rented a limousine. Once again the taxpayers were on the hook.

Oda reimbursed the government for her excess expenses and was eventually forced to resign from Harper's cabinet. As in the case of Dingwall, Oda's glass of orange juice enraged people just as much if not more than the thousands of dollars she wasted on limousines and the accommodations literally considered suitable for royalty. Even people in the private sector who have liberal expense accounts would never think of expensing such things as chewing gum and orange juice.

But there were also meatier scandals during the Ford years, such as the one involving former London, Ontario mayor, Joe Fontana. Prior to being elected as mayor of London, Fontana was a 30-year professional politician and was a Liberal MP who served in the cabinet under Prime Minister Paul Martin. In 2005, while a cabinet minister, Fontana spent $1,700 in relation to his son's wedding and billed the government for it. He forged a document that showed payment to the venue was actually for a political event, not a private wedding. In November 2012, the mayor was charged with fraud under $5,000, breach of trust, and uttering a forged document. At the time, police said there was another improper payment to Fontana of $19,000 but there was not enough evidence to proceed on that charge.

Fontana pleaded not guilty and was found guilty of the three charges in June, 2014. He later resigned as London's mayor. The following month, the 64-year-old politician was sentenced to four months of house arrest to be followed by probation for 18 months. Although Fontana accepted the judge's findings, he claims it was all a mistake. He was IN-NO- CENT!

And then there was the scandal involving some members of the Canadian Senate. The Senate has strange rules in that in order to be appointed to the body, senators must represent a particular province and be resident there. But many appointees are MPs or more lately, members of the Ottawa press corps who, despite what province they hailed from, are resident in Ottawa or the surrounding area. This led to the temptation to indicate the property they owned in their home province as their primary residence even though they really didn't live there. These senators whose primary residences were more than 100 kilometers from the nation's capital were then eligible to receive a housing allowance for their Ottawa home.

The auditor-general of Canada became concerned about these housing allowances and other expenses claimed by some senators. The investigation into improper spending began in late 2012 and involved Liberal Senator Mac Harb as well as three Tory senators; Mike Duffy, Patrick Brazeau and Pamela Wallin.

Harb eventually resigned his senate seat while the other three left the conservative caucus. Towards the end of 2013, Duffy, Brazeau and Wallin were suspended from the Senate.

In some cases, the improper expenses went beyond the housing allowance. In July 2014, Duffy, a former journalist with *CBC* and *CTV*, was charged by the RCMP with 31 criminal charges including fraud, breach of trust and bribery. The bribery occurred as a result of a $90,000 payment made to him by Nigel Wright who was then the prime minister's chief of staff. The payment was allegedly made so that Duffy would have the funds to reimburse taxpayers for his improperly claimed housing allowance.

Other charges allege Duffy billed taxpayers for expenses that were personal or partisan in nature and not related to Senate business. It was also alleged Duffy claimed per diem expenses for Senate business during a 12-day period when he was actually vacationing in Florida.

Duffy is also alleged to have paid $60,000 in consulting fees to a friend who did little or no work. These monies were alleged to have been spent for personal gain and were paid outside of the normal senate oversight rules.

The fact that three out of the four senators were appointed by the Conservative Party of Canada meant there would be a lot of coverage in the media who do not even attempt to hide the fact they want to see Justin Trudeau and the Liberals in power. Canadians were inundated with news of how their money was misused by appointees to the upper chamber.

As bad as the crimes (Fontana) and alleged crimes (Duffy) at the federal level were, they paled in comparison to what was happening in Ontario under the Liberal government. EHealth was one scandal where over $1 billion was spent, much of it on untendered contracts. The province's auditor general found after this large expenditure, there was little to show for it.

If that wasn't bad enough, the interim CEO of eHealth stepped down in early 2014 because of family concerns. He was replaced by David Rounthwaite who had been the general counsel of eHealth. He also happens to be the brother-in-law of the premier. Even though he was probably qualified for the job, the decision reeked of nepotism.

And then there was Ornge that saw executives set up private companies while getting large salaries from the government and incurring extremely high expenses. All of this was done in the name of providing a better air ambulance service for the province.

The most egregious provincial scandal was that involving two gas plants that were under construction. The decision to cancel and relocate the two gas plants was a purely political decision by the government to save a couple of Liberal seats and cost taxpayers over $1 billion. Emails concerning the relocation were deleted from Liberal Party hard drives and at the time of this writing the Ontario Provincial Police are conducting a criminal investigation into the deletions. In late December 2014, the Liberal Party announced they would reimburse the taxpayers the $10,000 plus tax they paid to have these hard drives cleansed. The party is no doubt trying to impress Ontarians with paying back the measly sum of a few thousand while ignoring the $1 billion that was wasted for no other reason than the Liberals were desperate to save a couple of seats.

It seems like every time a financial scandal involving the province died down, a new one emerged.

MaRS is a public/private partnership to provide facilities for innovation and research. Begun in 2000, it now consists of two towers located next to Toronto General Hospital, just across the street from Queen's Park. Difficulties emerged over phase 2 of the structure that saw the province of Ontario pour more and more money into the venture. By 2014, the phase 2 tower was only 31% occupied. The American firm, Alexandria Real Estate (ARE) was about to default on loans made to it by the Ontario government. In 2011, the province lent Alexandria $224 million for the construction of phase 2.

Despite the large projected provincial deficit, the province decided to throw $309 million more into the project including money to buy out ARE. Ontario planned to increase the occupancy rates by moving bureaucrats into what is often described as a "white elephant."

Instead of throwing more money into the project, the government could have saved the taxpayers' money and simply foreclosed on the property when ARE defaulted. Instead they decided to use more public money to buy out the American firm.

As 2014 drew to a close the government announced they would inject another $86 million into the project. Despite the high rents that caused the building to remain largely empty, the government has convinced itself by putting in more money, the building will eventually become fully rented. To date, the Ontario Liberals have thrown $400 million of good money after bad. After the downturn in the economy and rents that were too high, the Liberals did nothing that would minimize the losses to the taxpayers of Ontario.

MaRS was mentioned in the 2014 Auditor General's Report. The auditor general, Bonnie Lysyk, found the value of payments for MaRS was "uncertain" and said the payments created the perception some of the funds were used simply to bail out an American company. These payments were found to be highly risky to Ontario taxpayers.

MaRS was not the province's only public/private partnership. There were a total of 74 of such projects. In her report, Lysyk noted the Liberals spent $8 billion more on these projects than if they had been carried out only by the public sector.

A major criticism of the auditor general was the province's smart meter program. Smart meters were installed in 4.8 million homes throughout the province and the cost to install each meter varied between $81 and $544. The AG found that the program cost $1.9 billion, almost double the initial cost of $1 billion.

The purpose of the program was to reduce hydro rates for people who used a lot of hydro during off-peak hours. Lysyk found bills of customers who used hydro in these off-peak hours did not see their bills decrease nor was the amount of power needed to be generated reduced. A shocking finding was that while the net benefit was estimated by the government to be $600 million, it was closer to $88 million. The AG found the Ministry of Energy neither updated the costs nor tracked them to figure out what the net benefit was.

Usually after an auditor general releases his or her report that contains evidence of over or improper spending, governments usually say they will try and do better even when they have no plans to do so. But that was not the case concerning the smart meter program.

Energy Minister Bob Chiarelli went on the attack saying Lysyk was wrong and did not understand the electricity system because it was too "complex." That comment was taken to be patronizing and sexist, implying the minister said it was too hard for a little girl to understand. The opposition immediately called for Chiarelli's resignation but the premier stood by him, saying he only had a difference of opinion with the AG. In his comments Chiarelli made no mention of the fact that Lysyk had worked for

Manitoba Hydro for 10 years before her appointment as Ontario's auditor general. This was a prime example of the total lack of concern the Ontario government has over how it not only spends but wastes the tax dollars received from hard working Ontarians.

The Ontario government exports electricity. The auditor general found between 2006 and 2013, the province incurred a loss of $2.6 billion in these exports. During this same time period, the utility's customers were forced to pay an additional $50 billion on top of market rates.

A billion here, a billion there, and the Liberal government did not seem to care.

No discussion of wasting tax money would be complete without the Pan American (Pan Am) games. The Pan Am games are modelled after the Olympics and involve sporting events involving countries in the Americas. The games are held every four years, the year before the summer Olympics take place.

The city of Toronto bid for the games in early 2009 when Miller was mayor and Dalton McGuinty was premier. In November 2009, the city was awarded the 2015 games. All three levels of government were excited after two bids to hold the Olympics had been rejected. It did not take long before some people were referring to the event as the "Pan Scam games."

Pan Am executives, many of them provincial Liberal appointees, showed they had a sense of entitlement. CEO Ian Troop was fired in December 2013. Troop, like all top executives was paid over $300,000 a year. He and others were criticized after expensing everything from traffic tickets, dress shirts, orange juice and a cups of tea and coffee at Starbucks costing $1.89. Alcohol was also expensed by these execs who often had expensive team dinners. The executives of the games also spent taxpayers' money on travel and often took out cash advances on their government credit cards, requiring the government to pay high interest charges.

Troop was not the only executive to leave. But he, as the others, did not leave empty handed. Troop's severance package, including legal fees and other monies for such things as health benefits, totalled approximately $500,000. It was David Dingwall all over again.

At the beginning of 2014, the executives and the Ontario government admitted the $1.4 billion budgeted for the games did not include the cost of the Athletes Village. To the Ontario Liberals, the cost of another $1.1 billion wasn't worth thinking about.

In her 2014 auditor general's report, Lysyk found the budget for security of $247.4 million had already doubled and would likely go higher. She accused the Liberals of under budgeting. While some of the increased security costs can be justified because of increased security threats from homegrown terrorists, this does not account for the entire increase in the budget.

These days no sporting event can be held without a mascot and the Pan Am games are no exception. The mascot for the 2015 games, Patchi the Porcupine, was designed by four Grade 8 students. After a contest, the students were found to have the winning design. An access to information request put in by the *Globe and Mail* found the mascot cost the taxpayers of Ontario $385,000. This figure included $33,250 for "mascot research" and $134,550 to pay the 17 actors who will wear the costume.

As the games will not be held until the summer of 2015, it is expected the costs especially related to security will go higher before the event is completed.

It seemed Torontonians were always having their taxes wasted, except in the city when Rob was mayor. If the provincial Liberals weren't using millions of dollars to locate gas plants for purely political purposes, federal MPs and senators were fraudulently claiming expenses they were not entitled to, charging taxpayers to travel and stay in luxury accommodations allowing them to quench their thirst on $16 glasses of orange juice. The Fords on the other hand, not only did not misuse taxpayer money on themselves, but often used their own money for things they properly could have billed the taxpayers for.

As noted above, when Rob was a councillor, he was criticized for actually spending his own money for office expenses. There was no accountability said the critics as if it was terrible for him to make city-related photocopies at Deco rather than bill the taxpayers for it. And it wasn't fair the Fords were rich and could do what many other politicians could not afford to do.

When Doug was first elected to council, he promised he would donate his entire salary to charity. Prior to the 2014 election, the Ford haters were screaming that he hadn't proved that he had done so. But the entire family is known for being heavily involved in charities and donating to causes.

As an example, Rob has been selling bobbleheads of himself, often for charity. In November 2014, these "Robbie Bobbies" were sold for $30 at the mayor's office. Ford, grateful for the medical care he received at Humber Regional and Mt. Sinai hospitals since first being diagnosed with cancer, said he would donate the proceeds from the sale of the bobbleheads to the hospitals.

While mayor, Ford cut down on the number of taxpayer paid junkets councillors took to other Canadian cities and other countries. Under previous administrations, an inordinate number of councillors would fly off to Europe on the taxpayers' dime to study how other cities were doing things. The same information the councillors were seeking could have been obtained through a Google search or at most a telephone call. Even if the trip could be justified, it is a mystery why so many councillors had to go to study the same thing.

On the rare occasion when Rob travelled outside the city on business, he paid his own expenses. And of course he was soundly criticized by the left for doing that.

Since first being elected back in 2000, Rob has always criticized spending by councillors. And his hospitalization didn't stop him from speaking out. As 2014 was an election year, the office budgets for councillors were set at $28,000 for the period from January to November. None of the 44 councillors went over their budgets.

Although the councillors all came in under budget, the outgoing mayor was not happy about the spending. After Ford began his third round of chemotherapy, he issued a statement criticizing how much was spent. He criticized the many councillors who spent very little at the beginning of the election year leaving the large amount of spending to later in the year when they knew these expenditures would not be made public until the election was over. Saying he was disappointed in what he saw, Ford vowed as the newly elected councillor in Ward 2, he would continue to fight any increase in the office budgets and expense accounts of council.

Not only did Ford not waste taxpayer money, but he never ripped them off like Fontana did or like Duffy and other senators are alleged to have done. He really did respect the taxpayers.

Members of Ford Nation were upset that the media spent so much time digging up dirt on the mayor while appearing to give the impression other frauds and wasteful spending was no big deal. It was simply business as usual especially in Ontario. The more the financial scandals played out, the more Ford's fans appreciated his preference to spend his own money and the fact he never personally benefited from their money.

It can never be said that Fords benefited financially while in office through fraud and payoffs to their friends. Members of Ford Nation realize this.

Chapter 11

There Were No Suitable Candidates
Other Than the Fords

Once the major candidates were all in place for the 2014 campaign, the media was essentially correct as labelling Chow on the left and the other four as on the right or centre right. Of course none of the other candidates were as fiscally conservative as the Fords.

It can be argued whether Stintz and Soknacki were on the right or the left but since their combined polling numbers had difficulty reaching double digits, it really did not matter if they were on the left or the right. The race from the outset was between Chow, Tory and Rob, later to be replaced by Doug.

Chow was a socialist tax and spender, the polar opposite to the conservatism of the Fords. For people who followed politics closely and held strong political views, if they supported Chow they could never vote for a Ford even if their terms in elective office had been scandal free. Likewise, no supporter who liked the Fords' policies could ever vote for Chow.

Tory was the only candidate acceptable to those who liked the Fords' fiscal policies but who wanted to end what the media constantly hammered home was the circus at city hall. Tory was the only choice for those who could not bring themselves to vote for a mayor (or even his brother) who smoked crack, appeared drunk in public and uttered comments that, if they were not racist, homophobic and anti-Semitic, they could certainly be interpreted that way. By the end of the race, Tory obtained the Anybody but Ford vote and was acceptable to many of those who consider themselves conservative.

Tory had been a Progressive Conservative all his political life. He was a lawyer and more importantly a businessman who surely would see to it that money at city hall would not be wasted. Tory comes across as a nice guy despite the fact he has a nasty streak that he showed in his disastrous 1993 election ad making fun of Chrétien's facial deformity. Another example of Tory being not so nice was when he also called on Rob to resign the same day the mayor returned to Toronto after finishing rehab. After finally admitting he had a problem and getting some help, Tory wasted no time in demanding he resign after he first returned to Toronto. Unlike Chow who attacked Ford mainly on the issues, Tory spent a lot of time attacking the Fords personally. But watching his demeanour and how he carried himself, it was hard to imagine Tory as mayor could ever turn into what the media would label a circus. And that was more important to Tory supporters and the media than saving money for Toronto residents.

There is no doubt Mayor Tory will be more prudent with the taxpayers' money than Chow would have been had she been elected. Had Tory not dreamed up his disastrous separate school funding idea during the 2007 election campaign, he may very well have ended up being Ontario's premier. If the PC's had formed the government, there is no doubt Tory would have been more concerned about the out of control spending and the growing deficits the province is accumulating than the current Liberals are and would have reigned spending in. For those who see themselves as small "c" conservatives but who are willing to settle for fiscal relativism, John was their boy. But it is impossible to imagine Tory being upset about councillors' budgets that are small in the general scheme of things or arguing about spending over $75,000 to water plants at city hall. And he would not have made the lowly hard-working taxpayer his main priority.

The political views among Progressive Conservatives runs the gamut from those who are true fiscal conservatives that want smaller government to those who are really indistinguishable from Liberals. Tory was in the latter group who are known as Red Tories.

Although candidates for municipal office in Toronto do not run under the affiliation of a political party, none of the candidates live in a political vacuum. Chow was a member of the NDP and Tory was PC but none of the candidates, even if Stintz and Soknacki are included, was a member or strongly associated with the Liberal Party. In government since 2003 and just coming off a surprise majority win in June 2014, a lot of Torontonians were supporters of the Liberal Party of Ontario. Without a party member running in the election, Tory was the main choice for those to who saw the Fords as too conservative and Chow as too far to the left.

While this factor helped Tory win the election, it completely turned off members of Ford Nation. On social media, many referred to Tory as "John Liberal." Tory picked up a lot of endorsements of well-known Liberals including sitting MPPs. He became buddy buddy with Wynne whom he previously ran against provincially and whose party his job was to oppose when he was the leader of the official opposition. Tory was too close to Wynne and the Liberals seen as being corrupt by many Ontarians to ever be the diehard choice of members of Ford Nation.

As to Tory's SmartTrack proposal, the main plank of his platform requires the electrification of the provincial GO train lines in order to work as Tory envisaged it. While the Liberal government has said they want to electrify these lines, they say a lot of things. Tory didn't seem to think this would be a big deal leading many to believe he has already obtained an agreement with his friend Wynne to electrify the tracks. This, coupled with the fact Tory's transit plan extends outside of the boundaries of the city of Toronto gave the impression to some people that in enacting his transit plan, he was simply complying with the wishes of the provincial government.

On December 1, the first day he came to power and a day before he was officially sworn in, Tory chose to meet with the Ontario premier. This reinforced the belief the newly elected mayor of Toronto is just a lackey for the Liberal government. If nothing else, it was a further indication of

Tory's major problem that plagued him throughout his political life—his lack of political smarts. Of course it is necessary for the mayor of Canada's largest city to get along well with other levels of government (Wynne refused to meet with Ford for over a year as a result of the crack scandal). But to visit her on his first day as mayor indicated to members of Ford Nation they were right; the former leader of the PC party's main priority was pleasing the Liberal premier of Ontario.

Throughout the 2014 election campaign, Tory kept saying he was the only candidate who was capable of working with other levels of government. Certainly, Rob had not been able to do that, especially after the crack scandal emerged and Wynne refused to speak to him. While it is necessary to work with other levels of government to get them to contribute financially on such things as transit, by constantly saying how well he would work with others, he gave the impression to Ford supporters that his idea of being mayor was to gather around the other levels of government and sing Kumbaya.

Tory's importance on working with others raised doubts to his ability to be a leader. A leader is someone like Ford who knew where he wanted to go if he was elected. Once elected, he attempted to get others to follow his agenda, the one that made him victorious. And he was successful at the beginning of his term in getting council to repeal the vehicle registration tax and contract out garbage in the west end.

Had Chow been elected, she would have led the city back to the days of David Miller. But at least she would have led. To members of Ford Nation, Tory at least gave the perception that working with others meant others, most notably the Ontario premier, would be calling the shots. One of Tory's main personality traits is a desire to be liked, not a great quality in a leader who is tasked with making tough and often unpopular decisions.

Unlike a government run by a political party where the leader must keep his or her caucus in check, the mayor has to work with people who hold divergent political beliefs. Many Ford supporters cannot see Tory, who has never held municipal office, coming out on top in the battles he will certainly have with long serving leftist councillors such as Pam

McConnell and former head of the Manitoba Communist Party, Paula Fletcher. The left on council are likely to walk all over him, destroying any fiscal responsibility he may plan to bring to the city.

Contrary to what the media may think, members of Ford Nation are not simply dismissive of Rob's use of crack and his other problems. But to Ford Nation, there was simply no other candidate able to carry out the Ford agenda that was still, despite the problems with Rob, a popular one.

Chapter 12

The Fords: Most Unusual Politicians

Even without the scandals involving the use of crack, the drunkenness in public and the making of statements that were racist, homophobic and anti-Semitic at worst, politically incorrect at best, the Fords are unlike any other elected officials. They are perfect politicians for those people who hate politicians.

As indicated earlier, Rob and Doug are two different people. One of Rob's strongest appeals is his personality. Other than small towns where everybody knows everybody else, what elected officials hands out business cards with their cellphone number on it and invites everyone to call if they have a problem? And when people called him, he would return their calls and do what he could to assist them with the problem.

Rob would do what he could to help people during his councillor days whether they were his constituents or not. And he didn't ask and didn't care who these people were. He would help those in subsidized housing where gangbangers and drug dealers live and would go help them as well. These are the type of Toronto residents that other politicians ignore and would not go near except to do photo-ops to show how much they care. No doubt, his contact with these unsavory people led him to smoke crack in public while in one of his drunken stupors. As many members of Ford Nation say, he's just one of us.

This became evident whenever Rob was out and mixing with ordinary people such as his trip to the Taste of the Danforth. Rob would be mobbed by people, and constantly posed for pictures with people. He had an attraction to people that went beyond that of simply being the mayor.

The Ford family is wealthy; their wealth coming from the success of Deco started by Doug Ford Sr. back in the early 1960s. The Fords of course are far from being the only elected officials to have money. Tory was born with a silver spoon in his mouth and achieved powerful positions in the private sector given to him by his father or his father's close friend, Ted Rogers. Which family has the most money is unknown but what they used their money for is different. The Fords put their own money where their mouths were and this set Rob and Doug apart from other politicians.

The Ford brothers, like other politicians, would fundraise during formal election campaigns. They would point out the fact that if someone donated $100 to their campaigns the person would receive a $75 rebate from the government. They would use any financial contributions they received, but if they didn't get enough money to fund what they wanted to do, they would just use their own money. This set them apart from other elected officials who nickeled and dimed the public. When Rob was mayor he would spend his own money on travel even if that travel regarded city business. The Fords would never think, like Dingwall and Oda, that there was no purchase too small to charge to the hardworking people of Toronto.

The willingness and ability to use their own money made the Fords distinctive and it is this factor that caught the attention of members of Ford Nation. "Respect for taxpayers" was not just a campaign slogan; it was the philosophy they used in governing and the concerns of the ordinary man and woman was the only interest they had.

Their feelings about the ordinary men and women of Toronto could be seen in the social event known as Ford Fest. Ford Fest was an annual barbeque Rob began after he was first elected to council. Initially held at his mother's home in Etobicoke, it became too large for her property and was later moved to city parks. During the 2014 campaign more than one Ford Fest was held. One was held in Etobicoke and another in Scarborough where, like the Fords' neighbourhood, showed strong support for the Ford brothers.

These Ford Fests were open to everyone and people entered long lines for hot dogs, hamburgers and drinks, all paid for by the family. The stars of the show were Rob and Doug, especially Rob who even showed up to one after his cancer diagnosis. People also lined up to have their pictures taken with Rob and Doug. Even the odd skirmish with protesters during the 2014 events did not dampen the day.

The willingness to use their own money meant unlike other politicians, they had absolutely no one to answer to. It is a reality of our political system that when major players make large donations or play active roles in campaigns, like it or not, these people feel they are owed something and take steps to collect.

The Ford brothers are and always were beholden to no one. When Rob was running for mayor before being stricken with cancer, Doug was his campaign manager. Although Doug did have a campaign spokesman, Jeff Silverstein, as Rob did, he pretty well ran his own campaign. Both Rob and Doug's campaigns are truly family affairs. They had no high profile political operatives running their quests for elected office as did other candidates.

Although it is unlikely no politician or other high profile person would have endorsed Rob in light of his admission having been drunk and using crack, the Fords never sought out endorsements. They didn't care. The brothers owed no one anything and they alone decided what they would do and how they would run their campaigns. All they sought was the endorsement of the voters at the polls.

Contrast that with other politicians such as Chow and Tory. Chow, a high profile member of the NDP was supported by unions and other special interest groups on the left. Had she been elected, she would have owed them and the unions and the other groups would have expected payback for their support. But Chow supporters paled in comparison to those who supported Tory in his successful bid to become mayor of Toronto.

Although the Liberal Party of Ontario did not endorse Tory, many of its members including MPPs did. These endorsements raised red flags that despite being a former leader of the Progressive Conservative Party, he would effectively be a puppet for the Wynne government, extremely unpopular with the province's real conservatives. Besides his ties to Queen's Park, Tory also has ties to corporations such as Rogers and Bell Media, raising doubts any priorities he has are those of the ordinary person.

Tory was the former CEO of Rogers and remained a member of the company's board of directors until days before he was sworn in as mayor. Tory also has connections to Bell Media that owns *Newstalk1010*, the radio station Tory worked for as a talk show host. Despite it being obvious Tory was going to run, he was able to use his radio platform to constantly criticize Rob before he formally entered the race and had to leave. Rogers and Bell own and control about 80 percent of the Toronto media. They were in the bag for Tory.

It is hard to believe Tory will not favour these companies over the concerns of the taxpayers in the same way Miller favoured the unions that supported him and was repaid with a lengthy garbage strike. The following is an example of what Ford Nation is worried about in the city under Mayor Tory.

In 2012, Rogers and Bell acquired a majority interest in Maple Leafs Sports and Entertainment (MLSE). MLSE owns the Toronto Maple Leafs, the Toronto Raptors and the soccer team, Toronto FC. In addition, the corporation owns a number of specialized sports TV channels.

It is far from unusual that owners of sports teams want new facilities built and look to all level of governments to pay for it. They use the canard that new facilities will mean more fans and more fans means more business for local entities such as hotels, restaurants and bars. It is difficult to imagine Tory could easily say no to this type of request. Again, this is only one example of Tory being asked for favours from his connections in the corporate world.

The Fords on the other hand have no such connections and no one they are indebted to. They did and Rob now as a member of city council will continue to put the taxpayers first above labour, corporate and other interests.

During their terms in office, the Fords did not care or pay any attention to the media. They served their constituents the way they wanted to no matter what the media, who in their cases were unmerciful, wrote or said about them. The Fords were beyond any and all influence and this fact alone endeared them to members of Ford Nation who chose to overlook the scandals and support the Fords who truly cared for the interests of the ordinary hardworking taxpayer. Not only were they not in it for themselves, they devoted all their energy and even their own money to carry out their program of stopping the gravy train and respect for taxpayers.

Chapter 13

Conclusion

To people living outside the city of Toronto and even those within its borders who do not follow municipal politics closely, it is hard to understand how anyone could possibly support Rob after all that has happened during his 10 years as a member of council and four years as mayor. While it is easy to see how fiscal conservatives support his mantras of stopping the gravy train and respect for taxpayers, it is difficult for those unfamiliar with Toronto politics to understand why he received continued support after admitting smoking crack in one of his drunken stupors and after having been videotaped making derogatory comments about gays, Jews and blacks. But they did.

The fact that a large group of people known as Ford Nation stuck by their mayor says more about other politicians than it does about Rob and his brother. These people, hard workers for the most part are sick and tired of seeing their taxes go up, government services reduced and their tax dollars literally wasted. They are sick and tired of having mayors who put the interests of unions ahead of theirs only to be rewarded by lengthy strikes. They are fed up with having their tax dollars used to open fancy offices in London to fight global warming and being told firearms should not be allowed to be manufactured or kept within the borders of Toronto. They are also fed up with having their lives micromanaged by politicians dictating what they can eat and whether their children can toboggan down a hill.

Members of Ford Nation are sick and tired of scandal after scandal involving their tax dollars. They are fed up with politicians who defraud them (Fontana) and who waste their hard earned money so they can live in luxury (Oda). They are sick and tired of governments spending over $1 billion for a pure partisan purpose (gas plant scandal) and spending more and more due to incompetence (Pan Am Games, MaRS) and to enrich consultants and their friends with very little to show for it (eHealth). They are simply fed up with how the political class act.

There is no doubt Rob and Doug are unusual people and even more unusual politicians. Rob especially in the way he gives out his cellphone number and attempts to help anyone who asks him to solve a problem they have. The Fords do not seek endorsements or money from corporations, unions and special interest groups. They accept campaign donations from individual residents and if they do not get enough to do what they want to do they use their own.

Rob is especially admired for his refusal to bend to the constant demands for his resignation and the constant criticism and name calling he endured since he first came on the municipal scene in 2000. A lesser man or woman would have given up years ago. But Rob persisted in order to pursue his objective of not wasting the tax money of Toronto residents. While the scandals are often used as an excuse, those who were constantly calling for his resignation did so because they hate him and his politics.

Although some people might think it's cool to have a mayor who uses illegal drugs and appears drunk in public, the vast majority of Ford Nation are law abiding people who do not approve of Rob personal conduct but support him in spite of his behaviour. They were willing to overlook the scandals because there were simply no other politicians who cared more about them than Rob and Doug did. These other politicians cared about themselves, their friends, and their corporate, union and special interest group supporters. Had another politician come along who had the same genuine care about taxpayers, things would have been completely different.

The first printing of journalist Robyn Doolittle's book, *Crazy Town*, ended with Rob formally entering the race for mayor in January 2014, eight months before cancer caused him to withdraw. Doolittle, generally detested by members of Ford Nation, opined that 20% of voters would vote for Rob in any event. She added another 20% liked his policies and if he could rehabilitate himself before the election he could not be counted out. While her numbers might be slightly off, Rob did have a chance of being re-elected had he been physically able to stay in the race. As indicated earlier, there were no incidents of Rob using drugs or being drunk in public after he finished rehab at the end of June 2014.

Warren Kinsella, a Liberal Party strategist, pundit and columnist who worked for a time on the Chow campaign, appeared on *CP24* during their election night coverage. Shortly after John Tory was declared the winner, Kinsella said both the Fords deserved to be humiliated. Instead, Rob won with a decisive victory in Ward 2 and Doug finished a respectable second in the mayor's race. He added Ford Nation is something Tory cannot ignore.

Doug is out of municipal politics and Rob's intention of serving out his term as councillor and running again for mayor in 2018 will be dependent upon his health. But Ford Nation is not simply a fan club for the brothers. It is a political philosophy of fiscal conservatism and respect for the taxpayer. Ford Nation is not going anywhere and Tory as well as politicians who consider running in 2018 ignore them at their peril.

Afterword

On December 2, 2014, John Tory was sworn in as mayor of Toronto. In sharp contrast with Don Cherry who placed the chain of office around Rob Ford's neck and then made cracks about pinkos four years before, Tory was accompanied by William Davis and Louise Russo.

Davis was the Progressive Conservative Ontario premier from 1971 to 1985. During the 1980s, Tory served as principal secretary to Davis as well as associate secretary of the Ontario cabinet.

In 2004, Russo was in a North York sandwich shop waiting in line to buy a sandwich for her daughter. An attempted mob hit took place and Russo was struck by a stray bullet. The bullet shattered her spine, leaving her confined to a wheelchair. The mother of three later started W.A.V.E.; Working Against Violence Everywhere. Through her community work, Russo and Tory became friends. Russo delivered a speech at Tory's swearing in and placed the chain of office around the new mayor's neck.

The day before he was sworn in as mayor, Tory made a well-publicized visit to Ontario Premier Kathleen Wynne, bragging later how well he can get along with other levels of government. After the crack scandal broke out, Wynne refused to meet with Ford. This pre-swearing in stunt confirmed the belief of members of Ford Nation that Tory is nothing more than a liberal puppet of the premier.

The new mayor literally hit the road running when he decided to immediately tackle the issue of gridlock on Toronto's streets. Tory announced there would be strict enforcement of the no-stopping bylaws on major downtown streets during the morning and evening rush hour. A blitz was begun to tow vehicles including commercial vehicles making deliveries to downtown businesses.

It is hard to find fault with this decision. Gridlock cannot be eliminated as long as one of two lanes on major downtown streets are blocked either by commercial vehicles or cars whose drivers stop during rush hour to run into a coffee shop to make a purchase. There was some criticism of this as being anti-business; preventing trucks from making deliveries. But this has to be done if gridlock is ever going to be eased. And the private sector will be able to adjust their schedules so deliveries are not made to businesses on major thoroughfares during rush hour.

Towards the end of January, Tory announced parking infractions against vehicles with out-of-province license plates will be strictly enforced. If an out-of-Ontario vehicle gets at least three parking tickets it will be towed. These vehicles can currently park with impunity because there is no way payment of these parking tickets can be enforced. According to Tory, many of the commercial vehicles that stop in no stopping zones in rush hour downtown are not registered in Ontario.

It is too early to determine whether this strict enforcement will continue or whether enforcement of no-stopping zones was simply a publicity seeking event and things will eventually go back to the way they were.

Tory was just as quick to begin breaking election promises as he was to get Toronto streets moving. During the campaign, the major candidates were all asked about contracting out garbage collection in the west end of the city. Both Tory and Doug unequivocally said "yes." Chow was the only major candidate against it, arguing that competition was needed between private and public trash collection. Within days of taking office, Tory backed away from the promise saying the matter of contracting out garbage collection east of Yonge Street had to be "studied."

Not only was his promise to contract out an out and out lie, but it makes no sense. When council first considered the privatization of garbage collection, they limited it to the west end of the city. Either it saved millions of dollars a year or it didn't. While Tory is the new kid on the block the city has the figures on the savings made through privatization. There is really nothing to study.

There is nothing inherently different between picking up garbage in the west end of Toronto and collecting it east of Yonge Street. To Tory's critics, there was no reason for this reversal other than Tory's wish to pander to the city's unions. This decision does not bode well. Miller's placing the wellbeing of the city's unionized workers over taxpayers resulted in labour disruptions that saw garbage rotting all over the city during the hot summer months. Rob on the other hand had no great love of unions but was able to give Toronto four years of labour peace.

After breaking that promise, breaking other promises came as no surprise. Although the city's 2015 budget has not been passed in city council at the time of this writing, Tory set out what he wants in his first budget.

During the campaign, Tory promised public transit fares would not increase during the first year of his term. In a quick turnaround, the new mayor announced he wants to see a 10 cent increase in Toronto Transit Commission fares. He used the familiar excuse those on the left use; the financial situation at the TTC was far worse than he thought. He also announced something quite unexpected. He wants children 12 years of age and under to be able to ride Toronto's transit system for free. There has never been a hue and cry from Torontonians that children be allowed to take transit for free. Seniors and those with disabilities of course will still have to pay.

No doubt giving children a free ride, pun intended, is part of Tory's plan to do things "for the children," a major plank in Chow's campaign. If this passes, we now have the situation where lower income residents; those who must take public transit back and forth from their minimum wage jobs will have to pay 20 cents more a day while children of millionaires can travel free. Tory said he regretted making the promise of a fare freeze.

Tory justified the 10 cent fare increase by saying it was necessary to restore service cuts to bus routes undertaken during Ford's term as mayor. In doing so he took swipes at the "previous administration," hoping everyone is blaming those cuts on Rob.

It seems Tory never stopped to consider that while Rob introduced the service cuts to some bus routes, these services were only cut after a vote in council. Many of these councillors who voted for the cuts were re-elected. He is criticizing some of his council colleagues with whom he wants to sing Kumbaya. It was not the wisest of moves but he's never been hailed as being particularly politically astute.

During the election campaign Tory also promised to hold property tax increases to at or less than the rate of inflation. Chow was the only one who promised to hold taxes to "around" the rate of inflation. While there is no theoretical limit as to how high inflation can go, that gave her a lot of latitude to increase property taxes while keeping her pledge.

At the time of his announcement, the rate of inflation was slightly less than 2%, mainly due to the large drop in the price of oil. At that time city bureaucrats were using 2.6% as the official rate of inflation for the city. Tory broke another promise by introducing a tax increase of 2.25%. While below the city's inflation rate, that figure has to be added to the 0.5% increase passed by the last council to fund the Scarborough subway. The resulting increase of 2.75% is not holding property taxes to even the exaggerated figure the city of Toronto uses. Another promise quickly down the drain.

Changes to the province's rate of assessment will effectively increase property taxes by 0.45%, leaving Toronto homeowners with an effective increase of 3.2%. While out of the control of the municipal government, there is only one taxpayer and this taxpayer will be looking at a property tax increase that exceeds the rate of inflation.

In addition to the increase in property taxes, Tory wants to increase user fees homeowners are required to pay. The cost of the city's small garbage bins will increase by 29 cents a month while the cost to property owners of the largest bins will rise by about $6.00 a month. This was done with the goal of reducing waste produced and the added cost to those, especially people on fixed incomes seemed of little or no concern to the new mayor.

Water rates have increased by 9% for the past nine years in order to pay for infrastructure and the replacement of decaying pipes. These increases were scheduled to end in 2014 but have now been extended. Residents will see their 2015 water bills increase another 8%. While less than 8% increases are scheduled for future years, they are not etched in stone and can be further increased.

Using the language of progressives, Tory said these increases are needed for "investments" in the city

During the election campaign, Tory seemed unsure of many aspects of a key promise, his SmartTrack plan. Not to worry. Tory got his executive committee to agree to spend $1.65 million to study the plan.

If ever there is proof that the gravy train the Fords tried so hard to stop is up and running at full speed again, it is in the area of council salaries and expenses. The new mayor wasted little time in announcing increases that will personally benefit him and the 44 members of council.

Councillors' salaries will increase by $2,649 a year to $116,562. And their office budgets will be increased by $2.5% for a total annual budget of $33,997.

Tory's budget calls for the mayor's office budget to increase to $2.2 million, an increase of 17% over 2014 that was higher than it should have been because it had to be split between Rob and Deputy Mayor Norm Kelly who assumed the duties council took away from Ford. The amount Tory wants is $800,000 more than the mayor's budget was in 2012 when Rob and his staff had full control.

The increase includes the hiring of additional staff to bring the total compliment of those working in the mayor's office to 20, an increase from the 17 staff members in the Ford/Kelly administration.

Despite the increase in property taxes and user fees, Tory's budget has a deficit of $86 million. Rather than attempt to look for savings in the budget in order to balance it, the mayor went running to his friend Premier Kathleen to bail him out. In what must have been surprising to the mayor who likes to brag about how close the two are, Wynne said "no."

Wynne, much more politically astute than Tory, has to be seen as not favouring Toronto over the rest of the province. If she bailed out the city, not only would it cause resentment in the rest of the province but she would be expected to do the same for other municipalities.

The province did however agree to give the city a $200 million line of credit that Tory quickly accepted. The guy who claimed to be Rob Ford without the circus said it was the best he could do.

The line of credit is secured by property and carries interest.

While Tory's actions to date were expected to draw criticism from fiscally conservatives such as members of Ford Nation, the new mayor was also taking flak from left wing councillors. Some criticized the line of credit as being risky. At least one thought property taxes should have been increased a further 3% in order to get rid of the deficit.

After Tory was criticized by the left, he reversed himself and decided not to take line of credit. He chose to use the city's reserve funds to make up the shortfall.

The *Toronto Sun*, the newspaper that bills itself as "conservative" came out with an editorial criticizing the budget as not being tough enough and criticized him for appealing to the left wing on council. Only three months previously, the same paper ran an editorial saying it was "Tory time" because he's a consensus builder and of course not a Ford.

During the first two months of the new administration, it is easy to feel sorry for Olivia Chow who for half a year led the polls until her campaign tanked. Fiscally, Toronto would probably be in the same position as if she became the city's chief magistrate. No privatized garbage collection west of Yonge Street, tax increases above the rate of inflation and free transit "for the children." But these things are consistent with her campaign. She could have implemented Tory's budgetary agenda without breaking any promises.

Tory is only two months into his four year term as mayor so it is difficult to predict exactly what will happen during the coming years. But so far he has proven Ford Nation to be correct in their characterization of him; he is not the fiscal conservative many of the "Anybody but Ford" voters supported because they thought he was not a tax and spender. Unlike many politicians, especially the Fords, he has a strong desire to be liked and constantly brags about how well he can get along with others. He very likely will try and please everybody and end up as a one term mayor who pleased nobody.

As the 2018 municipal campaign rolls around, a lot of people are going to want a change. If Tory continues to act as he has during his first two months as mayor of Toronto, the voters on both the right and the left will want change.

If Rob's health holds up, he cannot be counted out as being the next mayor of the city of Toronto.

About the Author

Arthur Weinreb is the associate editor and columnist for *Canada Free Press*, formerly *Toronto Free Press*. He has written thousands of political columns for these publications, as well as for several Internet sites. Weinreb is the coauthor *of A Criminal Lawyer's Guide to Immigration and Citizenship Law* and the author of *Racism and the Death of Trayvon Martin*.

Weinreb is a retired lawyer who practiced primarily in the fields of immigration and criminal law. He lives in Toronto, Canada.

Made in the USA
Lexington, KY
21 April 2015